Investigative and In-Depth Reporting

INVESTIGATIVE
AND
IN-DEPTH
REPORTING

by
Judith Bolch
and
Kay Miller

COMMUNICATION ARTS BOOKS

HASTINGS HOUSE · PUBLISHERS
New York 10016

Excerpt from TO HELL IN A HANDBASKET by H.
Allen Smith. Copyright © 1962 by H. Allen Smith.
Used by permission of Doubleday & Company, Inc.

Library of Congress Cataloging in Publication Data

Bolch, Judith.
    Investigative and in-depth reporting.

    (Communication arts books)
    1. Reporters and reporting.   I. Miller, Kay,
joint author.   II. Title.
PN4781.B58   070.4'3   77-21100
ISBN 0-8038-3413-6
ISBN 0-8083-3414-4 pbk.

Published simultaneously in Canada by
Copp Clark, Ltd., Toronto
Printed in the United States of America

Contents

Preface   vii

1. **The New American Hero:**   1
   An Introduction to Investigative Reporting

2. **Half Cop, Half Poet:**   13
   Characteristics of the Investigative Reporter

3. **The Outs Versus the Ins:**   21
   Origins of Investigative Story Ideas
   Beat—Tips—Known Tipsters—Anonymous Tipsters—Intuition—Patterns—Files—Stories Leading to Stories—Two Case Histories

4. **Filling in the Blanks:**   41
   Sources of Information to Develop the Story
   People—The Beat—The Principal Figure—Off-Beat Sources—Other Reporters—Social Functions—Law Enforcement Officers—Peripheral Sources—Association Experts—Records—Public Records—Other Records—Libraries—Files—A Case History

5. **Drafting the Battle Plan:**   59
   Controlling the Interview
   Self-Control—Preconception and Fairness—Demeanor—Controlling the Interview—Getting In to Talk—Identifying Yourself as a Reporter—Beginning the Interview—Asking the Questions—Listening to the Answers—Handling the Liar—Keeping the Mike—When to go "Off the Record"—Controlling the Situation—A Case History

6. **The Litmus Test:** 83
   Deciding When a Story is Justified
   On the Basis of the Subject—Something Reportable—
   Families of Officials—"There's Always Something"—On
   the Basis of Evidence—Is It a Story?—Shun Salvage
   Operations—Can I Prove It?—Two Case Histories

7. **Trial Balloons and Other Four-Letter Words:** 102
   Recognizing the News Manipulator
   Organized Manipulation—News Conferences—News Re-
   leases—News Secretaries—Other Types of Manipula-
   tion—Including the Reporter—Trial Balloons—Being Set
   Up—Executive Sessions—Threats—Higher Reasons—En
   Garde!—A Case History

8. **Of Pots and Kettles:** 127
   Ethics for the Investigative Reporter
   Reportorial Arrogance—Conflicts of Interest—Invasion of
   Privacy—Invasions by Questions—Invasion by a Side
   Door—A Case History

Index 143

Preface

When we were journalism students, the available textbooks never went much beyond defining the inverted pyramid or musing about the mass media in lofty terms. Those textbooks—and the great majority of the ones on the market today—miss the point of the daily activity in newsrooms of papers and broadcasting stations. Emphasis was on news writing, rather than on news gathering. Professors who had been reporters in their youth occasionally offered anecdotes about how they had tracked down sources or obtained material for a story, but these were isolated tips.

Then, as novice reporters, we gradually acquired the quite unmagical tricks of the trade both on our own and through observation of and discussions with veteran news people. No experienced reporter or editor can lay it out *in toto* for a newcomer—the practitioner is too busy doing to take time to teach.

Although effective reporting is in large measure a matter of instinct, timing and talent rather than of acquired skill, many useful techniques can be learned through example instead of trial and error. Requiring every newcomer to stumble along by himself until he learns a trick here or hones an approach there is a waste of the reporter's time, the news organization's investment and can cost both of them botched stories as he learns his craft. How much wiser to help the novice turn himself from a person who basically knows how to say something into a person who has something to say, i.e., a reporter who has competently collected the facts for a story.

This text focuses on the one point in a reporter's working life when he is beyond the assistance of editors or colleagues: the period during which he is pursuing the information on which to base an article or broadcast. A poor writer can rely on the expertise of others to lead him through the labyrinth of transforming rough copy into readable prose. But no one will be there to help a less-than-skillful interviewer face a reluctant source or to tell a confused researcher what to extract from a pile of possibly pertinent facts or to provide guidance in making the ethical choices sometimes involved.

That's why we wrote this book. We have collected these guidelines to speed the way for other beginners, to show him or her how others have handled the problems inherent in the nature of investigative or in-depth reporting. This book is not for the person who lacks a rudimentary grasp of the basics, but is intended for the student who wants to pursue topics in more than a cursory manner.

We wish to thank all the reporters and editors who shared their ideas and experiences. Hearing the story behind the story is one of the best parts of being a journalist anyway, and these case histories bring together dozens of suggestions about the practice of our craft. What worked for these reporters will, in most instances, work for others.

JUDITH BOLCH
KAY MILLER

Raleigh, North Carolina
December, 1977

Investigative and In-Depth Reporting

1

The New American Hero:

An Introduction to Investigative Reporting

*"There is mighty little good
in a mere spasm of reform."*

Investigative reporting: avenger of the wronged, illuminator of the corrupt. Exposer of the past, analyst of the present, harbinger of the future. Conscience of those governing, consciousness of those governed.

To the uninitiated, investigative reporting bears these exotic connotations. That two *Washington Post* reporters could, in the 1970s, weave wisps of information into a rope strong enough to snare the President of the United States is heady stuff, imbuing with glamour a field more characterized by patient drudgery. Before the Watergate burglary and the ensuing scandal, investigative reporters had rarely reached such national and international heights. And certainly the craft of reporting itself had never become part of the story as it did in this case, leading not only to Pulitzers for the reporters who uncovered the news but also to plaudits for their account of how they had done it. A new American hero had been born, and students who wanted to follow in the footsteps of Bob Woodward and Carl Bernstein filled the journalism schools. ("The Missing American Hero Turns Out To Be . . . Clark Kent," an article in *New York* magazine claimed with glee. Its cover showed Superman jumping into a phone booth, proclaiming "This is a job for a mild-mannered reporter," and emerging as Clark Kent.)

But investigative reporting predates Woodstein, as the pair of reporters came to be called, and it will go on long after them. This book examines the investigative reporting field as practiced by the media throughout the United States, and through the words of experienced editors and reporters presents a how-to manual for would-be journalists. Here are case histories and examples drawn not from imaginary worlds but from the backgrounds of men and women who have succeeded as investigative reporters. No one can turn overnight into a reportorial knockout merely by reading a book, and this text does not promise to send a student immediately on his way to *The New York Times*. But the experiences and achievements of others can offer guidelines to save the novice from at least some of the wrong turns he is certain to take. Furthermore, exploring the subject from the viewpoint of media members provides an assessment not only of "how," but also of "why." No one can speak more incisively of the motivations and challenges of investigative reporting than the reporters themselves. And no one else is better qualified to answer the ethical questions surrounding this topic.

Investigative reporting, as practiced by the weeklies in West Virginia, the dailies in California, in radio and television newsrooms, and elsewhere across the nation, does command attention and may right some wrongs. But on a day-to-day basis, it does not hold the public spellbound nor the reporter in a paralyzing grip of fear for his well-being. In short, it is both less and more than the movies make it out to be.

Investigative reporting differs from routine reporting mainly in degree of thoroughness. While all reporting utilizes the same basic tools (questions, interviews, research), these weapons are wielded more skillfully for an investigative piece.

It is vital that the term "investigative reporting" be broad enough to include the concept of articles other than the exposé. The exposé implies wrongdoing on the part of an individual or group, the existence of an evil situation for which someone is to blame. Certainly investigative research is needed to compile stories on such topics, but equally arduous research may be necessary to produce stories which do not reveal immoral or illegal actions but do uncover situations which need public attention. The term "investigative reporting" must, therefore, be considered applicable to any story which 1) deals with a serious subject, 2) involves obstacles which make gathering information on the subject difficult, and 3) fully explains or explores the significance of the subject. For example, we can say that while the average article reporting the opening of a new private club for blacks would scarcely require investigative reporting, this, like many subjects, *could* be appropriate for an investigative piece. A *Washington Post* article took that night club, examined the sociological and economic issues at play, and ended up with a fine investigative piece.

Similarly, as a recent article in *More* pointed out, investigative reporting weakens itself if it concentrates overly much on politics and ignores the private sector. This article argued that the immense influence of "business" cannot be ignored and that decisions made in the nation's boardrooms are just as important as those made in Congress. What went on in David Rockefeller's bank, for example, probably equalled in significance what was occurring in his brother Nelson's vice-presidential office. We do investigative reporting—and journalism—a disservice, therefore, if we perceive its limits too narrowly.

But let newsmen speak for themselves about what investigative reporting really is.

"Investigative reporting is nothing in the world but good reporting," says one experienced investigative reporter. "Now there are nuances that come in, I'll concede that. Investigative reporting requires more documentation than a lot of the run-of-the-mill work because you are frequently dealing with a person's livelihood, with his reputation, more than in a routine news story. You have to be much more careful of the damage you can inflict and that makes you cautious. It makes you look for any additional back-up material you can find—documentation, verification from other sources if you can't find it written."

A nationally-known editor pinpoints several traits needed

to successfully carry out an investigative article. "It takes more patience and persistence. You are tied up with records. The payoff is much further down the road. You work day in and day out without ever having anything in the paper. It's like putting together a crossword puzzle. It takes time. It takes time."

The lack of glamour was underscored by another nationally known editor. "Good reporting is 99 and 44/100ths per cent sweat. If what you are interested in is the once-in-a-lifetime thing, a scoop that puts the federal judge in jail, you come upon that only by accident. And it is the payoff for hours and hours of just good hard routine sweat work. It's the same for police and detectives. I am sure they don't operate the way we think Sam Spade does. I am sure most police work really is patient drudgery. And most good reporting is patient drudgery."

One editor notes that investigative reports sometimes have innocuous beginnings. "Very frequently what turns out to attract headlines as investigative reporting may have started out not to be investigative reporting at all. Just turned out that way. Sometimes you think you are going to do some investigative reporting, and it turns out there isn't anything worthy to qualify under that term," he says. "But it's all basically reporting."

One former investigative reporter notes that if a newsman likes to see his byline daily, then he won't be interested in investigative work because it takes longer to produce a complex article. "Just as *All the President's Men* demonstrated, it's getting people to talk. All reporting is like that, but investigative reporting is more so. You have to have a talent for eliciting information from people, getting them to have confidence in you and knowing how to ask questions."

An editor, who spent many years as an investigative and political reporter himself, feels the only difference between routine reporting and investigative work is its intensity. "All good reporting means is getting all the facts you can get, or all that are meaningful, and telling them. What we've come to think of as investigative reporting normally means that the facts aren't lying there on the table. They are not readily available; there are obstacles of various sorts lying in the way. It's a digging assignment.

"I think we've come to look at investigative reporting as reporting of official corruption and scandal, but I think that's a misconception of what investigative reporting is or ought to be. Good investigative reporting may be examining bad conditions or exposing an issue, and it has nothing to do with anyone going to jail and in many ways it may be a more fruitful kind of investigative reporting than sending a highway commissioner to jail for illegally taking money. Simply putting a guy in jail, while it cleanses the governmental process and is exciting because it's like one-on-one competition in basketball, puts no end to this process as long as you have scoundrels. Occasionally one will get elected to office and you hope you'll expose him and get him out of office, but as far as your impact on your constituency, you may contribute something longer lasting and more worthwhile by the kind of issue-oriented investigative reporting than you could through scandal hunting.

"I am not saying we shouldn't investigate the scoundrels," he cautions. "The thrill of the chase is more fun to do, and the other is more dreary, drudgery work and the results aren't as dramatic, but for the average newspaper which is not going to take on a President very often, the editor of that paper ought to be looking at not just the problems of scandal and corruption, but at the problems of his area and investigate those problems and expose them to the public."

Another reporter vigorously agrees, saying that he never really cared about those things his paper seemed to define as investigative reporting. "I wasn't interested in going out and finding the bad apple in the barrel, finding the crook and sending him to prison. To hell with that. If every newspaper had an investigative reporter fulltime who turned up one crook a month in state government for 20 years, I guarantee you there would still be plenty of work for the next 20 years because one crook is simply replaced with another.

"My whole point was, and still is, that investigative reporting deals with issues and conditions rather than incidents and events. The newspaper tends to be incident- or event-oriented. Well, I think that's wrong. They have to be to some extent, of course, because they are daily, they have to be current.

But far too little of their energy goes into the trendy kind of story, the long term, the kind of condition that might have existed for a long time, the institutional wrongdoings, determining if an institution is functioning for the benefit or detriment of society. I try to deal with those things."

Investigative reporters do make a difference in the quality of life they find around them. While scoundrels are a continuing part of the scene, surely the most outrageous among them do need to be toppled. Spotlighting conditions that need changing may improve circumstances on a more permanent basis. But investigative reporters are not usually faced with the choice of pursuing either Story A or Story B. Story ideas or leads come to the reporter's or editor's attention, and they are examined as they surface. It would be a rare investigative reporter who, faced with a lead on a political bribery story, would say "No, I prefer to do pieces on welfare fraud or rural health conditions." Drew Pearson and Jack Anderson made their careers from political investigative reporting. If one particular milieu appeals to the individual reporter, he can work into that specialized field. However, investigative reporting usually is a mixed bag.

One investigative reporter is dismayed his work does not have permanent effects. "I can see that some of what I did produced tangible results, but it bothers me that there aren't many examples. For instance, when another reporter and I did a series on abuses in absentee balloting in the mountains, I doubt that anyone would quarrel that changes occurred in the administrative procedures in the state elections office. I think there was clearly a tangible impact there, certainly short term. I did another series on the coroner system, and I think it encouraged counties to take advantage of the enabling legislation that had been passed previously to drop the coroner system in favor of the medical examiner.

"But beyond these two specific examples, I can't think of anything else that stands out. It's possible that stories I did on the Ku Klux Klan, or hunger or prison reform may have made some impact, I can't say. I can't say the conditions in prisons got any better because I don't know. There was no immediate change in the law, which is the one area where we can measure our impact.

"My main justification is that it has a cumulative effect. If we were doing it at our paper, maybe somebody else would get interested too. We were influencing someone else. I can't tell you that all the years of work had specific impact. Looking back, I've tended to become a little jaded after losing 40 per cent of my stomach from ulcers that went along with the decade I worked on that paper. Was it worth it, all those years to work my ass off? Fifteen- and eighteen-hour days were routine for me. Was it worth it? Well, I don't know. I look at it now, and, by God, you look at the legislature that was in session this past year and you say to yourself, 'Jesus, all those ten years when I was in effect slugging away at the legislature and trying to make my state, my home, where I live, a better place, and it really hasn't amounted to a hill of beans. Yesterday's newspapers are wrapping fish, and the people forget easily, and what the hell, it wasn't worth it.'

"But investigative reporting is part of the newspaper's function, and if it doesn't do such reporting, it's a living lie."

The contributing editor of a national newspaper echoes these thoughts and agrees with the "cumulative effect" theory. "Revealing the salad oil scandal resulted in jail terms and changes in the Securities and Exchange Commission. We had a series of stories on interlocking directorates which resulted in changes in the law regarding those. We had some judges removed in Illinois about ten years ago. I suppose if you are human, you will be disappointed if your story does not make a concrete change but is just dropped on a growing pile of similar stories. I don't think you ought to be surprised. Most stories, with rare exceptions, are just one more on the pile. When laws get to be changed it's not because of any one reporter's story. It's a cumulative thing. It's not true that Woodward and Bernstein would have impeached the President, if he had been impeached.

"Even in his leaving office, they made a contribution, but many other people did too. It's very, very rare that one story can have that kind of effect. But what the hell. Is that the reason you are in the business? Because it won't happen to one out of a million. And very frequently some of those stories come from some of the worst reporters you ever saw, and their only claim to any sort of (professional) respectability in their whole life is this one home run which they lucked into for some reason.''

Investigative reporting loosely might be considered to have begun in the early days of this country, when a newspaper served as propaganda sheet for a particular political party. Although the papers usually dealt in vitriol rather than in investigative work as we know it today, they also probed the lives of politicians in the other parties. Jefferson's party paper, for instance, pursued Alexander Hamilton as he pursued a Pennsylvania woman. Hamilton, not content with denying the charges in the paper of his party, subsequently wrote a book telling his side.

An example of investigative reporting more in line with today's concept is the assault by *The New York Times* on the political chicanery of Boss Tweed in New York in the late 1800s. A reporter named George Jones wrote about the corruption, and Thomas Nast's cartoons drove the points home. The muckraking era brought attention to the reporters, many of whom were utopian reformers, as well as to their probes. Lincoln Steffens, Ida Tarbell, Upton Sinclair, Ray Stannard Baker and Burton J. Hendrick are names well known for being in the forefront of the muckraking era, when scandal, corruption and vile conditions were exposed in meatpacking, railroading, big oil, banks, Wall Street, Congress, insurance and the poverty of the human condition. Principal vehicles for these articles were the weekly magazines such as *McClure's, Collier's* and *The American Magazine* which paid premium salaries to attract top-flight writers. On the West Coast, the *Sacramento Union* fought the corruption and stranglehold of the Central Pacific Railroad.

President Theodore Roosevelt took note of muckrakers on April 14, 1906, at the laying of the cornerstone for the House of Representatives Office Building. The points he made then may well be heeded by investigative reporters today:

There should be relentless exposure of and attack upon every evil man, whether politician or businessman, every evil practice, whether in politics, in business, or in social life. I hail as a benefactor every writer or speaker, every man who, on the platform, or in book, magazine, or newspaper, with merciless severity makes such an attack, provided always that he in his turn remembers that the attack is of use only if it is absolutely truthful. The liar is no whit better than the thief and if his mendacity takes the form of slander, he may be worse than most thieves. It puts a premium upon knavery untruthfully to attack an honest man, or even with hysterical exaggeration to assail a bad man with untruth. An epidemic of indiscriminate assault upon character does no good, but very great harm. The soul of every scoundrel is gladdened whenever an honest man is assailed, or even when a scoundrel is untruthfully assailed.

Roosevelt, who coined the term "muckrakers" after the Bunyan character who saw only the dirt at his feet, also noted that "There is mighty little good in a mere spasm of reform."

The muckrakers of Roosevelt's day would be followed by people such as Paul Y. Anderson, who uncovered the Teapot Dome story of Harding's administration; Edward Bok and Mark Sullivan who wrote in *Ladies Home Journal* of the drug content of nonprescription medicines; Charles Edward Russell who identified New York's Trinity Church as a slumlord and David Graham Phillips who wrote *The Treason of the Senate*. Thomas Lawson also wrote of Wall Street excesses for *Everybody's Magazine*, and Samuel Hopkins Adams covered the patent medicine business in "The Great American Fraud" for *Collier's*. During the Great Depression journalists wrote about sharecroppers, miners, migrant workers, small farmers, blue-collar workers and the unemployed.

These reporters and articles were followed by I. F. Stone, who was forced to publish his own newsletter to get his stories out; Ralph Nader, who functioned as a reporter when he wrote *Unsafe at Any Speed;* Morton Mintz, who reported the dangers of thalidomide; Seymour Hersh, who uncovered the atrocities of My Lai; and the dozens of investigative reporters at work today.

One former investigative reporter says investigative reporting sets in as a tradition at many news operations and becomes *de rigueur*. "If a newspaper allows such reporting to go on, the new reporters assume the banner as the older ones leave. All the years I was there the newsroom had certain people who were writing the kinds of stuff that makes other reporters say 'Damn it, I wish I had done that story.' And then they say to themselves, 'Damn it, tomorrow I will do that story. Tomorrow I'll turn that phrase. If this guy can make his words sing a little bit, then, by God, tomorrow I'll make mine sing a little bit.' A good newsroom has got to have that, the continuity of work and example that just goes on and on."

After a brief fling, however, some newspapers abandon the investigative piece. "For one thing, it is expensive," says an editor. "It's the most expensive kind of reporting a paper can do. You assign a reporter or a team of reporters to look for something other than routine news. That's going to require a great deal of time, a good deal of research."

"I was lucky as a reporter," says another, "because I wanted to cover social matters, and most papers weren't concerned with that sort of thing. My newspaper was interested. But, my God, who would spend the time and money to crank up teams to go out and investigate hunger, for God's sake. Most weren't interested."

A former reporter, who is now an editor, concurs. "Many papers lack either the guts or the money to do investigative reporting. It is time-consuming, costly in money and controversial. Some newspapers don't want to get into it. Those that do have got to be reconciled to the fact that you dig a lot of dry holes, and every tip and lead does not automatically produce a story because of the nature of the thing. If it were lying there on the top of the table, everybody would be doing it so there wouldn't be any investigative story to do."

In short, investigative reporting is not new and it is not easy. It does not possess any one form. It may be one long article or a series. If a series, it may be daily or intermittent. It may cite corruption or scandal, but it is not limited to that. It may spotlight a trend or a condition.

It may, as did the award-winning stories done by one North

Carolina newspaper, span as much as 15 years. The reporter looking back on the articles he compiled on the environmentalists' fight against damming the New River asks, "How do you sustain a story for 15 years? There was never more than a two- or three-month period without a story on the New River. Sometimes there were daily stories for six or eight weeks." That momentum was maintained both by the complexity of the ever-developing story and because the paper traced its subject from every angle.

Often effective investigative pieces are written in the wake of a news story that seems to need more depth to make it understandable. One example of the latter was *The New York Times'* follow-up to a news story about a young New York girl whose baby was eaten by her dog while she was away from her apartment. It was a tragic story, but on reading it many people certainly wondered how such a thing could have occurred. Was she heartless? Why did it happen? Could it have been prevented?

A reporter sent to do an in-depth piece interviewed the girl's family and friends to form a picture of her early life and spoke to welfare people and officials of other agencies in Manhattan to learn how this girl had dropped through systems meant to assist people. The in-depth piece made the tragedy no milder, but it did explain how it occurred and perhaps helped avert similar situations.

Note that the last sentence said "perhaps." Reporters can only point out what needs to be changed. The Fourth Estate does not enact laws, make changes in regulations, nor take the culprit by the scruff of the neck and toss him into prison. Frustration is no small part of a reporter's life. He may write an impressive investigative series only to have it virtually ignored. He must console himself with the aforementioned "cumulative" theory of reporting and go on to other topics.

Two concepts propel him to do future stories. One is that the next story needs to be done—a bad situation exists and needs to be aired. Much like climbing the mountain, the story is written because "it is there." The other motivating factor is that while Watergates come along once (or less) a century, his story still could be the blockbuster that will make a difference in the way things are.

What does the future hold? Investigative reporting can't depend only on finding and cracking future Watergates, but it must continue to work on stories that are locally significant. The way such probes are conducted may change, according to one editor.

"I think we are going to learn, like other businesses, that when you need specialized talent you don't expect a reporter to do it. If you are working on a story about bank fraud, papers have simply got to go out and retain an accounting firm to work with the reporter. If you need a lawyer, you retain one. I think you'll see editors hiring investigators who can't write and then teaming them up with a reporter to do the story. You can't ask very many people to have expertise in wide subject matter and law and all of this stuff and be fast on the uptake and be able to judge people and be able to write too. We are deluding ourselves if we think we can make just any reporter into an investigative reporter."

For the time being, however, reporters are on their own. No teams of reporters, accountants and lawyers have been established yet in most of the nation's newsrooms. What is personally required of an investigative reporter? Who's the most likely to be effective? The next chapter reviews the characteristics cited by investigative reporters and their editors.

2

Half Cop, Half Poet:

Characteristics of the Investigative Reporter

*"I think that's the weakest part of 90 per cent
of reporting . . . the reporter doesn't
know what the hell he is talking about."*

"The basic motivation of newspapermen is that they are born gossips. They want to find it out, and when they find it out, they want to tell it as quickly as possible, and they want a reputation for being very reliable gossips."

So says a former *New York Times* editor who's now editor of a large Southern paper. He's right about that characteristic, but there are others just as important for an investigative reporter to possess.

This same editor lists what he expects of the people he hires: "What you look for more than anything else is enthusiasm, willingness to work and work hard. Because that's what it really is: hard work. Interest. A desire to know something about everything and to be able to see a story. A real desire for accuracy. To be right and be first. Competitive spirit. Energy, a lot of energy. All these things."

One investigative reporter puts it more succinctly when asked to define requisite personality traits: "Craziness."

He says, "You've got to be really inquisitive, curious. Just keep asking 'Why?' and 'What does that mean?' You have got to be crazy in the sense that you've got to be willing to go anywhere at anytime to do what you've got to do. When another reporter and I were working on one particular story, I got up two or three mornings in a row at 4 a.m. and drove all over this damned town, trying to determine where some of these guys we were checking into spent the nights. It was just a wild, crazy idea. We were looking at who stayed with whom because they had all these different apartments and different cars, and we were kind of staking them out to see who was going where and who was driving which car. It never panned out, but it was the kind of thing where if your editor says, 'This is what you got to do' and you make a face, then there's no point in wanting to be in it. But otherwise you say, 'Okay,' and go out and do it. It's a willingness to do things that might seem very boring to other people, like plowing through records a lot.

"It also helps if you are single or if you have a miserable family life. If you've got a family, and family concerns start getting in there, they kind of cut into your time. And you've got to be able to work long times at all hours. You can't work 9 to 5.''

Being an investigative reporter does not require a "tough" personality or a threatening manner. It does mean that you have to do what is necessary to get information. You ask the public official about his unusual expense accounts. You confront a politician with the harsh effects of his successful gutting of a bill in the legislature. You ask demonstrating groups how their actions are going to resolve their grievances. You question allegations made by people who've called a press conference. A person employed by a news organization can get by for a while lobbing easy questions to his subjects, but this dream world won't last long if the news organization is as aggressive as it should be. You ask for names, dates, places, specific instances. You don't swallow general condemnations, vague assertions; you require specifics. And when you ask, you don't flinch.

Too many reporters are intimidated by their subjects, virtually asking to be conned. To be a reporter of any kind, but especially an investigative reporter, means you won't be getting a lot of valentines. A reporter early on must come to terms with the realization that his sources are not his friends. To some reporters familiarity converts their sources into buddies, making hard questions impossible to ask. And, lest any reporter think he is "friends" with those on his beat, let either lose his professional position. The phone will stop ringing.

Government and those possessing other forms of power are naturally retentive, and the press is naturally extractive, as was once pointed out by former Ambassador Charles Bohlen. An investigative reporter has got to have the tenacity to keep extracting information.

A college degree is generally considered necessary today for beginning reporters. Arguments can be made against this requirement, particularly in those cases where the job candidate has wide experience in getting around the world on his own, a good mind and general maturity.

In the old days reporters were an exceedingly eccentric lot, getting to the newsroom by various routes and then picking up the trade from others. *American Heritage* in its August, 1967, issue reprinted excerpts from a short story titled "The Reporter Who Made Himself King," by Richard Harding Davis, one of the earliest and most famous reporters. Much of what Davis wrote applies today:

. . . Now, you cannot pay a good reporter for what he does, because he does not work for pay. He works for his paper. He gives his time, his health, his brains, his sleeping hours, and his eating hours, and sometimes his life, to get news for it. He thinks the sun rises only that men may have light by which to read it. . . .

After three years—it is sometimes longer, sometimes not so long—he finds out that he has given his nerves and his youth and his enthusiasm in exchange for a general fund of miscellaneous knowledge, the opportunity of personal encounter with all the greatest and most remarkable men and events that have risen in those three years, and a great fund of resource and patience. He will find that he has crowded the experiences of the lifetime of the ordinary young businessman, doctor, or lawyer, or man about town, into three short years; that he has learned to think and to act quickly, to be patient and unmoved when everyone else has lost his head, actually or figuratively speaking; to write as fast as another man can talk, and to be able to talk with authority on matters which other men do not venture even to think until they have read what he has written with a copy-boy at his elbow on the night previous.

Another aspect of education pertains to the reporter's area of coverage, or beat. Some reporters try to bluff. If they are covering the legislature, they report day-to-day occurrences, but because they don't have knowledge of the state's political history, alliances and legislative operation, they can't produce deeper stories. It is possible to get by this way. But if you want to move to a larger paper or to a broadcasting station in a larger market (in each instance that means a raise in pay), you had better have some depth. It is possible to do a sloppy job, collect a weekly paycheck and think that your face on the TV screen or a daily byline means you equal the crack reporter for another news organization. You may think that if you like, but it's the person with the moxie who'll be sought by larger outlets.

It might seem nagging at worst or foolish at best to mention the necessity for knowing what you are about when it comes to reporting, but there's been a tendency recently for new reporters to opt for this career because of its associated glamour. Take the ego trip if you like, but being an effective investigative reporter will take work. Yours.

One editor pointed out:

"Generally speaking, I think reporters today are better educated, more informed, more sophisticated, even perhaps more talented, in terms of raw talent. There's just one area in which they seem to fall short when compared with reporters of 10 to 20 years ago. They don't seem to be willing to work as hard. And by working, I don't mean just the reporting, but the background, maintaining interest, especially in improving themselves and improving their writing. I seem to recall, and I could be quite wrong, that there was more interest when I was a young reporter, much more interest in really working on your writing, and in knowing what's really going on than there seems to be today.

"Reporters today think they can learn from pure experience. They think they've got to duplicate all of history. You can't begin to understand a state's politics unless you've got some understanding of history. How, for example, can you explain the difference between our senator and governor, both of whom are Republicans, unless you know something about mountain Republicanism as contrasted with Goldwater Republicanism? All these things contribute to your background, to your understanding."

Another editor wryly specified that reporters should be literate. Unfortunately, many reporters today aren't. If they use words improperly, they convey an inaccurate impression to readers or viewers. Occasionally, the results may be merely amusing, as when a television reporter doing a political story combined clichés in "There are several candidates for lieutenant governor who have jumped on the political bandwagon by tossing their hats in the ring" or when another reporter told his audience that a prominent man's death had "stirred up a keg of nails." But such usage demonstrates that the reporter does not understand what he's saying, a practice which raises questions about his credibility.

Being literate does not require one to be a walking *Roget's Thesaurus* (although that trait does come in handy at times), but it does mean that the reporter can relate his story in an understandable way. An interest in words and expression is an asset for a reporter.

The ability to write carries with it the ability to be concise. One reporter recalls a story that illustrates that necessity. "A father was telling his daughter a bedtime story. The father rambled on and on and on. He told her about the color of the flowers and the shapes of trees and the landscape and on and on. Finally she looked up at him and said, 'Daddy, what's this story about?' He replied, 'About a bear.' 'Well, bring on the bear,' she said."

Along these same lines, an editor says that "It's not sufficient just to get the facts. You've got to take them and put them into context and give them meaning and also make them interesting, make a person want to read. Because, you know, we can fill up the newspaper every day with facts but if nobody reads them we've lost."

"It helps if the reporter has some education and the more broad and varied it is, the better off he is," says another editor. "I'm not convinced that a journalism education is better for him, but it does teach certain methods and techniques he would waste a lot of time later on having to learn. But it depends on what he will specialize in. If he's a political reporter, for instance, and he has a broad background in history, political science and journalism, it will help him to do a better job."

Addressing the question of whether a journalism school background is useful, a reporter said, "I think it's a hell of a lot more important for a young person coming into journalism, instead of knowing what year the penny paper in Baltimore was founded, which is what many journalism courses tend to teach, to have a feel for the English language and to know a little something about English history, political science and such. I would suggest a course in government, because that's a reporter's meat and potatoes; government constitutes about 60 to 70 per cent, I would guess, of any reporter's day-to-day work. Second to that would be economics because, my God, government and economics go hand in hand. This training should be backed up with the English literature to help him with his writing and history, to tell him where he's at, in comparison with where we've been and where we're going.

"You do need an education to be an investigative reporter. By education I don't mean six degrees or a Ph.D or union card or journalism degree. As a matter of fact, I have recommended to many young people that they not even bother with a journalism school, unless they want to learn editing. If they want to be a mechanic in the newsroom, to shovel words together and hone phrases down, journalism school is fine."

One investigative reporter urges others to read. "Read not just one newspaper because you obviously can't get all you need from one, but read several. I think the more you read—newspapers, magazines, books—the better off you are."

An editor summarizes this idea with the adage: "To bring

back the wealth of the Indies, you have to take the wealth of the Indies with you.''

A former investigative reporter, who's now editor of a Pulitzer Prize-winning newspaper, says, "The keys (to being a good investigative reporter) are an analytical mind, the ability to logically deduce what happened if you are trying to fill in the blanks. You've got to be persistent. And, there's got to be a certain amount of righteous indignation present because sometimes exposing people gets very touchy. You are sometimes ruining a man's life; you are probably hurting his family, and you have to have enough righteous indignation to motivate you to go ahead and do what you have to do, rather than when you get a guy in a crack, simply folding your notebook and going home.

"You've got to have some understanding of what the role of the press is, and that is to seek out the truth. And you have to feel that is worthwhile. You've got to feel that if your facts are right, and the guy is in a pickle, you didn't put him there, he put himself there. So you have to push on.''

Another reporter sums it up by saying, "A good investigative reporter can't function unless he has one thing: the jugular instinct. But he has to have the wisdom to know when to use it and when not to use it. And you use it rarely, only when you absolutely have to. You have to be able to get around asking that direct question if it's at all possible. You can't just come slashing right in; you run people off. You ease into people, whether they are primary or secondary sources or the person himself. You ease into it.''

Accuracy is also essential. "A lot of reporters are sloppy in their methods and that's how errors come in. But if someone can be a good observer and doesn't let his own visions cloud him, and if he can write factually, accurately and lucidly about what he sees, and he has some comprehension about what he is doing, then he can be a good reporter,'' a newsman says.

One reporter who specializes in political/governmental coverage adds, "You can't go in there and just hack around, because you can screw it up. What if you are wrong about what you write on a political campaign and the guy loses? How do you fix it?''

One final point is in order here. Don't become so much a part of your job that you forget you have other responsibilities as a person and a citizen. Zealousness can go too far. Harrison Salisbury, former associate editor of *The New York Times*, recounts an incident which reveals the dangers of becoming too committed to reporting. Admitting that he belonged to the ''tough agency school of news reporting,'' Salisbury says that when he was a reporter in Chicago, a colleague was tipped that gangsters planned to murder the mayor on the steps of City Hall. The tipsters promised the reporter 10 minutes' notice so he could get to the scene for an eyewitness account. ''It never occurred to any involved,'' Salisbury says, ''that we had any obligation to tip off the mayor or the police about what was supposed to happen. The story was the thing.'' (By the way, when the mayor was later killed under other circumstances, the reporter who'd received the tip swore he had been double-crossed.)

3

The Outs Versus the Ins:
Origins of Investigative Story Ideas

*"Almost never do stories begin with
some reporter saying, 'I am going to go out
and investigate So-and-So, that crook.' "*

A stack of copypaper sits idly next to your typewriter, presumably waiting to be graced with a Pulitzer Prize-winning investigative report. But what to write about? Experienced reporters realize story ideas abound; indeed, sometimes the problem is to decide which is the most promising to pursue.

When a would-be investigative reporter complains about a lack of stories, the problem probably rests with his ability to hook a story idea as it glides by in conversation or his ability to synthesize something he heard two weeks ago with a random reference made today at lunch. For instance, one newspaper's series on a charity's finances arose after the reporter who did the obligatory promotion piece on the charity's upcoming telethon wondered aloud how it was possible that last year's telethon supposedly cleared only $700. She wondered, but wrote the expected piece. Another more alert reporter, hearing her comments, began a probe of his own. The resulting exposé caused the removal of the charity's director and top officials. Clearly, one reporter was "tuned in" to the possibility of a story; the other, even while it crossed her mind, ignored it.

While story ideas come from virtually anywhere, many investigative reporting pieces have origins that repeatedly produce stories.

Beat

The most usual place to find ideas is on one's beat. The day-to-day coverage of a particular institution, such as the sheriff's department, or of a specialized area such as education or health, can lead the reporter to short, event-oriented stories and to the in-depth investigative pieces. Someone on that beat may take the reporter aside and say, "Did you hear about . . . ?"

Most often, however, the reporter's knowledge of his beat will permit him to spot a story idea. One editor says having a beat is of inestimable value in producing stories. "You know the little cracks and corners and where the bodies are buried. You learn how to get the information you want." To this end, it is imperative that the reporter does in fact know his beat. Frequently, reporters share daily cups of coffee and chatter with sources on their beat without actually understanding how the agency functions.

A scenario was mapped out by an editor in which the alert reporter thoroughly learns his city hall beat. "He'll have to start covering the beat immediately, because newspapers tend to throw people in cold. But he will learn how city hall works by finding out what the duties of the mayor are in this particular town, what the duties of the police chief are, what the relationship is between the chief and the mayor, what the aldermen do and how they get elected, how they like one another and what the laws of the city are. He'll try to learn the business of city hall.

"Now a good part of this will seem in the beginning to be not very useful. But he'll develop understanding. And it often happens that in the process of learning he comes across areas in which he can go down and say 'Now the city hall or the board of aldermen are not doing what they are supposed to be doing,' " the editor says. Handling the beat's daily event-oriented stories may be possible without this knowledge. Using the beat as a source of ideas worthy of investigative treatment demands, however, an in-depth approach.

The problem, of course, is that close acquaintance with people on a beat may cause the reporter to forgo a story on the grounds that it's not new to him. Or he can get too chummy with people on his beat, regarding them as his friends and hesitating to check out items which might damage the friendship. Reporters who regularly covered the White House, for example, were willing to ignore the Watergate burglary and dismiss it as a routine police story. The existence of a White House tie-in seemed so farfetched that they hesitated to anger their political sources by pushing or probing. They feared they would alienate contacts and gain nothing. Woodward and Bernstein, unencumbered by White House relationships, were not afraid to let the story take them where it would. They had nothing to lose.

A story cited by a former *New York Times* reporter illustrates the additional danger of becoming so identified with sources on a beat that one forgets he is a reporter. During the 1960 Presidential campaign, he says, "One of Virginia's top political reporters and I were standing at the Capitol talking with Governor Lindsay Almond. Almond began to sound off to us about something Nixon had done, saying it was a backhanded means of dragging the Catholic issue into the political race. This other reporter just kept standing there. I started taking notes, and we had a front page story in the *Times* the next morning. Sometimes reporters get too comfortable and feel like they are just gossiping with ol' Joe, who just happens to be the governor, when it's actually news."

A beat can be an energizer, but it can also become a soporific, if the reporter isn't careful.

A former editor, mentioning the ways stories often begin, scotches the Hollywood version. "Almost never do stories begin with some reporter saying, 'I am going to go out and investigate So-and-So, that crook.' Stories begin because a reporter, covering a certain area of Congress or some aspect of government or business, sees a larger issue. Or else they can occur when one reporter notices something going on in his community, with the schools or a tax fight or whatnot. And somebody else says, 'You know, I wonder if the same thing is occurring elsewhere?' And so our staff looks into it. It might turn out that seven or eight reporters are ultimately involved in tracking down the information needed, but the story still began with one staff member who had an idea or mentioned something that clicked with someone else.''

Tips

Tips from known sources or anonymous ones are another way of getting leads on possible articles.

Investigative reporter Jack Anderson allegedly maintains a whole network of tipsters, and other reporters with established reputations have discovered that ''results breed results.'' One such newsman says, ''Almost any time you have a story in a certain area of government, you build up momentum. If you have the reputation, or if you have a series of stories exposing something, then you find that people will call you to say, 'If you think *that's* bad, let me tell you about so-and-so.' Then you are off and running again; there is a tendency for investigative reporting to feed on itself.''

Now we will discuss tips from known sources.

Known Tipsters

These are people you are acquainted with, whose credibility you can assess. Frequently they will have a self-serving motive for giving a newsperson information. As one experienced editor puts it, ''I take it for granted that anybody who gives anything has got some reason for doing it other than brotherly love.''

That understood, it does not necessarily taint the validity of the information provided. The ''outs'' are in a position to have a good grasp of what the ''ins'' are doing and from their past experience comes an ability to spot questionable activities. When they tell a newsman to investigate the background of a policy or project, they may be doing so because of self-interest, but the story which may result can be newsworthy.

When Elizabeth Ray made her revelations about Rep. Wayne Hays to *The Washington Post*, for example, she had a book ready for marketing and she very much wanted the publicity as an entré into the world of movies and televison. Despite her self-serving motives, however, her exposé of the fact that a congressman was paying his mistress with public funds deserved to be heard.

"I would take a tip from the devil himself if it was a story," says an experienced political reporter. "It's not inconceivable that sometimes the public interest and the private interest of someone else may coincide with a story. If the tip from an opposing politician leads to a good story or exposes real corruption, use it. In politics, particularly, there is a constant battle between the reporters and the politicians. Your aim is to use them more than they use you. You have to walk the tightrope the best you can, remembering they have the same goals."

An executive ousted by a large public utility, for example, served as the prime source for an exposé of its political slush fund. The man obviously sought revenge; yet the paper was adequately convinced of the validity of his accusations. He retaliated for his firing, yes, but at the same time the public learned of illegal corporate activities. One reporter who dealt with him says, "I never took a psychology course; I wish I had. Knowing where a person stands in relation to what you're doing is going to determine how you approach him. This man had a lot of motives; he had been canned by his company; he felt he had been treated very badly. That made him much more receptive than his former employers who wanted to keep their public image shiny."

As a general procedure, don't let a government official who's been fired or eased out due to patronage changes leave office without being interviewed on both an on- and off-the-record basis. You're interested not in just what he might say for publication but also in the inside story he can often give you about how things are actually being done in his agency, about who really has the power. Even if he's not mad enough to want revenge, he often will be more honest than usual. Ask him what a reporter should examine in his field: "If you were going to steal, how would you do it here? What would you keep your eyes on if *you* were covering this beat?"

Not only do reporters use the "outs" for information, they cultivate the "outs." Because people have different ideas and different ways of achieving their goals, someone will always be grumbling. There are "outs" in corporations, universities and associations. If a reporter has a business or economics beat, he will soon learn about politics in fights for control of corporations and disputes among top officials about whether this is the proper time to introduce a new product or propose a branch office. "Outs" can be found everywhere. John Dean became an "out" when he realized he might find Watergate hung around his neck by other presidential staff members.

Another type of known tipster can be the person who is genuinely interested in an incident or trend. This person may offer only the briefest snippet of information. It is up to the reporter to see what can be developed.

Although such an event rarely occurs, a newspaper applauds when someone comes in with the tip, the facts, and all the detective work done. That's how one editor received a story on a corporation's secret attempts to start strip mining operations.

The editor recalls how it happened: "This corporation was operating very quietly, going around the county taking soil samples. One day this geologist was driving along a rural road and saw overhead a helicopter with some sort of meter hanging down beneath it as it crisscrossed the area. He knew, since he was a geologist, precisely what was being done, and he checked with his industry and mining friends to find out who was over here messing around. He did the work for us, too, bless his heart. He marched all over the county and found where they were digging these cores to take for analysis. He would take the leavings from the spot where they'd taken the core sample, and he'd take some back to his lab and analyze them himself, trying to determine what they were after. He had been a consultant to several mining companies and was very familiar with strip mining.

"He came direct to us and dumped the whole thing right in our laps. If it hadn't been for his seeing that helicopter and running the story down, they probably would have been out there with the bulldozers before we found out about it. Instead, the corporation never had a chance to get established before we began running articles on what they were doing and on what strip mining does to woods and streams.''

It may occasionally happen that a person phones in with a tip, not realizing that there is more to the story than he thinks. Take Robert Redford's speeding ticket, for example. Or, more precisely, the fact that he did not get a ticket. He was stopped in Charlotte, North Carolina, for doing 67 in a 55-mile-per-hour zone. He did not get a ticket. The officer's wife, thrilled because her husband had seen Robert Redford in the flesh, called *The Charlotte Observer* to report the glorious fact. She never realized that other people might not think it was so wonderful that Redford wasn't ticketed when John Doe would have been. The paper ran the story, and the police department was deluged with so many irate callers the nonarresting officer finally wouldn't take any more calls.

Anonymous Tipsters

It's tantalizing to think that one day an anonymous letter will turn up in the morning mail and lead to a terrific article. But rarely do anonymous tips develop into worthwhile stories. They must not be immediately discounted, but they should be examined carefully. People with a personal gripe feel they can embarrass or coerce their enemy by getting a newspaper to declare a crusade in their behalf.

One reporter heard from an anonymous source after writing a series of articles on the Ku Klux Klan. The wife of a Klansman did not approve of her husband's belonging to the group, and she told this reporter she would give him information. "I had never met the woman," the reporter recalls, "and we spoke by phone for about six to eight months before I ever did get to meet her. But she would tell me things her husband had told her about what had happened in the meetings. I would take her information and check it against other sources I had. I'd compare the data. For several months I knew what was going to happen before it did. Ninety per cent of the information she gave me would match what I had picked up elsewhere. So I'd

write that 90 per cent.'' Another reporter picked up information
on a brewing financial scandal among several savings and loan
institutions by striking up a conversation with strangers in a bar
one night.

Intuition

Reporters occasionally divine stories because a piece of information clicks with something else stored away in the back of
their minds. You can't build a reputation waiting for such intu-
itive flashes, but it's interesting when they pay off.

An investigative political reporter describes how he pursued a story on the basis of a hunch. Note that he did not let
a secretary block him and that he approached his sources by
working from the outside to the center of the story.

"I heard about this thing called the Commission on the
Status of Women. I always have a suspicion about federal grant
programs, I don't care what they are doing. Some of them are a
waste of money. I had been poking around in the manpower
programs and had stacks of stuff but didn't know what the hell
was going on in them—they are so bureaucratic. I came across a
grant to this thing. They were going to set up county coordina-
tors who would then set up county councils on the status of
women. Whenever I see the word 'coordinator' that is a red flag
to me. I began to wonder what was going on.

"I chatted innocently with the state director of this thing,
and she told me what a great job they were doing, and how she
had even hired a man. I made notes of what she said, but it just
bothered me. I don't know what it was. So I called her office
about three months later and asked for a list of everyone hired
as a coordinator—names, addresses, their salaries and their
responsibilities. The secretary said she couldn't do that. I said,
'Lady, I want it, it's public record.' I was mad with her and
I said, 'This is what I want and I am coming down to get it.'
And they got it for me.

"I looked at the list and said, 'Now, who are these people?'
It so happened the Republicans were in the governor's mansion
at this time. I saw a name of a woman from a certain westerly
county. Well, I had a list of the Republican county chairmen

and vice chairmen. There she was, vice chairman of her county. I checked another county. I thought her name was familiar and whipped out a list of 1974 Republican candidates for the state legislature. There she was. Ohhhh. There's another woman on the list, and her husband shows up as county manager down east for the gubernatorial campaign. So that was three, real easy. I began to wonder what was going on. I checked out the party registrations of about 20 or 25 people on this list. Some were, in fact, Democrats or unregistered. But I found a lot of them who changed parties on November 8. Another woman changed on November 6. So I went to the Manpower Office where their employment records were. One woman was typical of all. Their first inquiry to her was November 1; she changed to Republican registration November 8; they hired her November 9. I found several like that. They were changing to Republicans. My editors weren't that gung-ho, but the federal law says these jobs are not to be used as political patronage whether partisan or nonpartisan. And there were never any set qualifications for hiring people. It was a very amorphous program, and I was on target but I didn't have any hard evidence.

"I did have sufficient circumstantial evidence to call these women. I told them I was doing a story on these councils, and asked them to tell me what they did. And I'd ask how they got interested in this. And they'd say, 'Oh, I inquired.' And then I'd say, 'Let me ask you something . . . how come you changed political party registration?' And they would go, 'Well, uh, uh, blah, blah . . . I, uh, just felt like it, I always liked President Ford.' I got the same type answer from everyone I called.

"The word filtered back, of course, to the director of this thing. You get nine innings you know, and I had used my first four or five as warmups, kind of batting the ball around. By the time I saw her, I had gone over my questions so many times that I knew to ask what seemed to be innocuous questions which would connect at the bottom.

"I asked her what she looked for when hiring these people, and she said some things, and then I asked her specifically how a couple of women got on the council. 'Well, she's a good friend of mine,' she said. 'Did you know her from politics?' I asked. 'Oh, we're just good friends . . .' And it went on like this. 'You've got women who changed party registrations.' 'I didn't pressure anybody,' she said, 'they did it of their own accord,' and she went on and on. At one point I said, 'Did you talk to anyone in the governor's office about these jobs?' She said yes. And I said, 'How about the governor's top political assistant?' and she said, 'What's he got to do with it?' I knew I was on the right track. You try to ask innocuous questions that are really very important in a very calm manner.''

Patterns

After being on a beat for awhile, a reporter will notice occurrences that are more than coincidental. A pattern may become apparent in a judge's sentencing, or in land purchases, for instance, or perhaps year after year the same charges of election fraud are heard from the same counties. These patterns will inspire articles.

In one case, for example, a reporter noticed a prevalence of verdicts of ''prayer for judgment continued'' from certain judges. That disposition allows a defendant to leave the courtroom freely without judgment, although if there are further violations he may be returned to court for sentencing. The PJC seemed to be especially popular with judges when the defendant was a prominent citizen. To substantiate that hunch, the reporter went to court records to determine exactly how many PJC's were being issued by particular judges. He talked with the judges involved to seek their reasoning behind the rulings and with other judicial figures to see if an unusual situation indeed existed. His story, which originated because he pulled together isolated incidents, resulted in a tighter law on the use of the PJC in that state.

Files

One former investigative reporter feels his own files were a good source for stories. ''I began building a file on money in politics back in 1963, way before it became a fashionable topic. I don't recall what triggered my idea that this might be a good topic but I must have noted an odd contribution that shouldn't have been. Maybe I did a story on this one time and dropped it. But meanwhile I launched a file on the entire subject and kept feeding it for five years. Everything that pertained to money or questionable use of money in elections I tossed into a manila folder.

"And, if I was sent to one part of the state to do a story on something else I might remember that I'd want to see some old political wheeler-dealer and I'd drop his remarks into the file. I kept picking on it. When I finally did the story the only thing I had to invest in it was about two or three weeks of active work to update some things and follow through on some others. There was one week of writing, and I had a 14,000-word series on money in politics in 1968 when it wasn't hot yet to talk about the funding of political campaigns."

Among things to save in your files: government reports and stories from your own newspaper or other publications on a subject you think you will want to delve into sometime in the future. If you are a political reporter, save campaign and administrative press releases, speeches, lists of campaign workers and appointments. Positions taken today, supporters today, change tomorrow. Also keep campaign advertising—newspaper ads and such. In these campaign publications, emphasis shifts, and not all changes are innocuous. Do keep campaign funding reports, although copies of these should be available from the files of the State Elections Board.

Stories Leading to Stories

One investigative political reporter recounts how he recognized a story idea which others had never pursued. Doing the first story led him to others.

"It had always been said in my city that politicians gave blacks money to buy their votes and get the vote out on election day. Well, I don't believe you buy the black vote anymore, at least not in the urban places. They are too sophisticated to say 'I know you want me and it will cost you ten grand for my support.' But the blacks do want money because they have an organized system to get the vote out—drivers, poll workers, babysitters for mothers to go vote—and they need money for gas. In effect, what they say is, 'Look, you give us the money and pay us for one day's work and we'll get the vote out for you.' You've got to make that distinction or else some people are going to say you are buying the black vote.

"There are some questions about it, but the candidates themselves organize their own 'Get Out the Vote' committees. Usually candidates try to use volunteers. Anyway, it had always been rumored that the blacks got money, and it dawned upon me that there is now a law that requires political committees to file reports with the State Elections Board. I know some blacks who were active in politics, and they admitted they had gotten some money in the last election but wouldn't tell me who it was from.

"I went to the State Board of Elections and asked if they had a report from this black committee and they handed it over. No one had ever looked. I picked it up a year after it had been filed, but if I had been in the office on election day the year before, there it would have been. It said they got a thousand dollars from a congressional candidate, a thousand from a U.S. senatorial candidate and a thousand from a candidate for state attorney general. Right there. The law had just gone into effect requiring this reporting, and they were obeying it. They reported who had given the money and how they had disposed of it. The whole thing. No one had ever looked.

"My story said that the get-out-the-vote effort a year ago was fueled mainly by money from these three candidates to this committee, and I was very careful to say that this was not illegal. But I did note that this was the first time such money has ever been publicly disclosed.

"But that story led to a whole lot more, because I said, 'Okay, let's see now how the politicians report *giving* the money. The committee had said they got it, but the politicians have to report that they gave it. They did some fast scrambling to cover their tracks, because the committee was not listed on their reports, but they said they gave it to an intermediary to turn over to the committee. The intermediary's name did appear on the list, but who knows if that's really this committee's money that was listed. There were cracks in their stories, but they stuck by the idea that they were reimbursing this intermediary.

"Anyway, this led to still another story. It dawned on me that if this committee had filed, there must be other committees like it. There was one called the 'Committee for a Two-Party System,' made up primarily of black Republicans. They hadn't filed anything, never did so. Then I decided to check from the other end and thought up some black Republican candidates, checked their reports, and there was a fellow who got $1,000 from this committee. I came up finally with about $6,000 or $7,000 in contributions this committee had made but not reported. I wrote that they had violated the law, and they had. The committee never got prosecuted, however, because the D.A. in that county said it was frivolous. But those stories all came about through curiosity."

Important pieces often are developed also from brief news items. Don't forget to examine the daily news for occurrences which deserve broader treatment.

TWO CASE HISTORIES OF HOW THE REAL STORY WAS INITIALLY IGNORED

It is not infrequent for a reporter to write an article which in itself is true but which misses a more significant point. (*The New York Times'* initial dismissal of the Watergate burglary as a common police story is a classic case.) In each of the following examples, other people were acquainted with the basic facts but did not develop the potential.

In the first instance, a reporter for one newspaper read an account in a competing paper about a company which had been awarded the state's advertising account for tourism and industry. His colleague had touched the surface of the story but had not been alert to what he was putting on paper. The second reporter, tipped off by a letter, was not so quick to dismiss the situation's implications.

The second account is summarized from the *Columbia Journalism Review,* January/February 1975. Note that the Omaha Sun Newspapers' managing editor, Paul Williams, took a well-known subject but uncovered its ramifications. Previous tentative passes at doing the story had been rebuffed by Boys' Home public relations people, and the paper had let the idea die aborning. This time the paper didn't give up. The subsequent Sun Newspapers' probe of Father Flanagan's Boys' Home won a Pulitzer Prize and resulted in changes at the institution.

Case Number I

"In the fall of 1974 there were some rumblings about the state advertising contract. It has always been a political football, at least since the 1960s, when the winning gubernatorial candidate gave the contract (which was worth about half a million dollars annually) to the firm that had handled his campaign advertising. And there's probably nothing wrong with that if you have a good campaign firm. Why not give it to them?

"But there are some problems in that the executive who runs the firm can go right to the governor if he doesn't like what his boss in state government tells him and you have those kinds of hassles. In this case, however, there really wasn't a firm. What happened is that the guy who did the governor's ad work formed his own company after the election and then farmed out the stuff to what was purported to be an independent firm in Florida, but which was actually his own company down there.

"There had been some rumblings about the way the firm was conducting its operation. The state auditor's office did an audit, and they found a lot of overcharges and undercharges, and they had some other questions. They put it all in the audit which came out in mid-1975. The highlight of the audit was that a very high-ranking gubernatorial aide took a Super Bowl trip, using two tickets the ad agency had gotten as part of an ad that ran in *Esquire*. In effect, the state wound up buying the two tickets which wound up in the governor's office and which then wound up in this guy's hands, and he took one of his women out to the Super Bowl. There was some question whether the state was paying for a free trip for one of its employees. So that was the highlight of the story as it was then, and another paper released it.

"Well, we got a letter at my paper from somebody who knew what the hell was going on, and it said if you look into

A-B-C-D you will find that this is what is really going on, signed 'Anonymous.'

"The letter more or less laid out everything. It just told us where to go. And it said that if we would compare statistics for several years, we would find that fewer people are responding to our state's ads, etc. I suspect that someone in state government really had it in for the guy who won this advertising contract.

"Another investigative reporter and I set out to find out what we could. He started looking over invoices, and essentially we were operating on the theory that the North Carolina firm was a shell, which is what it really was, and when its owner said he was subcontracting out to the Florida one, basically he was giving his buddy down in Florida the business. But they were the same people and they were adding a layer of profit or charges—a commission and then that guy farmed out the actual work. So in effect it was a double-billing situation, and it was right there. What we had to do was say how can we prove that both companies are one and the same?

"We worked independently, this other reporter and I. We knew something was there and things were funny. We made a whole lot of phone calls. I knew a girl who worked in state government in the department that this advertising comes under, and it turns out she was the ad guy's girlfriend at one point. She told me about him. We checked our clips and records on him. We were gathering a lot of information, and the other reporter saw patterns to the billing that suggested it was double-billing. Billings are public record. We got them from state officials. Then the other reporter went to Florida to look over the Florida records in the secretary of state's office and to see the actual offices of the ad firm down there. We were constructing a kind of history of the firm. He was looking for things like motor vehicles registration or occupational licenses. All sorts of stuff. Anything he could find.

"It turned out that the company here had about three different names and in Florida it shared the offices with the same company they were supposed to be subcontracting this work out to. In effect, it really smelled. We needed to find some kind of link.

"He came back from Florida and we found occupational licenses for the firm here and the one in Florida signed by the same guy, who listed himself as an officer in both companies. (Not the top guy, but his chief partner.) So there was our first tie-in. So our second tie was under our damned noses all the time. I found it . . . and it was right in our offices, too . . . which we didn't find out until after the story ran, but I had found the information somewhere else. I was over at the state department and I talked to another official who said, 'Look, blah, blah.' He said the whole thing is a mess and started telling me. And I said, 'Look, this is what I am looking for, a connection between this top guy's firm here and the Florida one. And this guy said, 'You know, when he first got the ad contract we had this big meeting of state officials to award it, and he had that partner guy up from Florida and I swear that he was introduced as his senior vice-president. Of the same company.' And he said it might be in the minutes of the meeting. And I looked in the minutes and there it was. The whole background of the North Carolina company, this guy. They came to the state and opened up and said, 'I am So-and-So, and here is my senior partner, Mr. So-and-So.' He was hyping them. He never really had anything. It was just a secretary, a front, and he farmed all the work out. But there it was. And when I got back to the office and after the stories ran, another reporter who was cleaning out his files came across these minutes in his files. There it had been! Right in our own office!

"We also had some lucky breaks. One key element of this story was that they were linked together; therefore, we were able to say the state was being double-billed. Another key aspect was that there were some blatant violations of the contract. It said you shall only get commissions on such and such, not such and such. They didn't have good bookkeeping. It was sloppy and just so blatant it was not just ineptitude. It seemed like it was fraudulent. The other aspect is that still another state employee secretly owned stock. The way we found that out, one of our court reporters happens to have some good ties into that political circle. She drinks with them, and one night they started talking about it and this fellow said, 'I did some legal work for this company' and then he told her that there was this silent partner in there who was a state employee who had his stock in a blind trust. So she came back and told us.

"The governor had no idea that this employee owned the stock. I really believe that. A lot of people suspected that the aide who went to the Super Bowl had a tie into it too, but we were never able to find that out.

"It also turned out that the silent partner's sister-in-law was a bookkeeper in the ad firm. You've got to know the names of people and who they are. In effect, you gotta know who they sleep with."

Case Number II

Father Flanagan's Boys' Home—more familiarly, Boys Town—is one of those lucky institutions whose national image for decades discouraged skepticism and pointed inquiry. As its latest fund solicitation letter says, it is "an independent charity for disadvantaged youths regardless of race or creed." Boys Town is far more than that. . . .

In Omaha, hometown to Boys Town, you notice also that the place has grown from modest beginnings into a sizeable institution—one, moreover, which has grown while conducting its financial operations in almost total secrecy. . . .

On a weekly newspaper, you have to try to find a few original ideas every week or month, a really good one once or twice a year. . . .

At Warren's (Warren Buffett, the board chairman of the Sun Newspapers of Omaha) home one evening in July 1971, we drank Pepsi, discussed the paper's progress and resources, and considered what new projects we might undertake. It was at that session that we decided to try the Boys Town story. The idea then was simply to report how the institution raised and spent its money. The public, both nationally and locally, had a right to know how its donations were being used.

Monsignor Edward J. Flanagan had started "the city of little men" in 1917, using an old mansion near the center of Omaha. In 1921 it moved to a farm ten miles outside the city. . . . Immediately after World War II Father Flanagan started a major building project: some $10 million worth of new dormitories, schools, a stadium and field house, industrial training shops, administrative buildings. He died in 1947, less than a year before the project was completed and dedicated.

For all practical purposes, that was the last big capital expenditure Boys Town had made. Yet each spring and again before Christmas, Boys Town sent out a lot of letters asking for money.

In the 1960s we had made a couple of tentative passes at the Boys Town story. The public relations people, the assistant director, and the director, Monsignor Nicholas Wegner, turned us down cold. "We just don't discuss our fund-raising program" was the general response. "It takes a lot of money to care for a thousand boys.". . .

It was also clear that we would have to start working around the edges, accumulating a core of information that would let us go back to the Boys Town leadership with hard questions. The possibilities broke down this way:

• As an incorporated village under the laws of Nebraska, Boys Town was required to file a condensed annual municipal budget and a brief report of operations.

• Boys Town had its own U.S. post office, acquired, apparently, for publicity purposes early in its life. It therefore had to file certain minimal public reports with the postmaster general in Washington.

• As the operator of a school system accredited by the state of Nebraska and the North Central Association, Boys Town had to make some reports of attendance, staffing levels, curriculum, and compliance with health and safety rules.

• Father Flanagan's Boys Home, Inc. was a nonprofit corporation under Nebraska law. It had to file very brief reports, primarily lists of officers and copies of the articles of incorporation, in the statehouse. Its status also meant that donations were deductible from income taxes.

• As a licensed child-care operation, it had to file other routine reports with the state Welfare Department.

• Because it owned land, there would be records of deeds and mortgages, taxes, prices, and transfer dates.

To begin the spade work, we chose Doug Smith. . . . We told him to go to the public relations director of Boys Town and anywhere else his nose led him, as long as he could explain his inquiries by saying that he was doing a general historical piece. He was to pick up all the handouts he could find, historical and current publicity pictures, and a general account of how the place operated.

Williams then describes how the reporters checked the post office, where an assistant postmaster noted that Boys Town got a tremendous volume of mail, and the statehouse. At the statehouse it was learned that Boys Town, despite printed claims to the contrary, did receive both federal and state funds. Educational records revealed that there were actually only 665 boys at the school rather than the 1,000 for which it was designed. Land records showed that the property was worth at least $8.4 million. The reporters also talked to enough people to learn that the Boys Town staff was very conservative and very tight-fisted. A check with an administrative aide to the district congressman revealed that in fiscal 1971 there had been 34 million letters mailed from the Boys Town post office; in 1970, 36 million; in 1975, 50 million. Fund-raising experts said a return of at least $10 million would be a conservative estimate for that amount of mail.

From the figures supplied by the school and welfare reports and from material supplied by national experts in child care, the reporters estimated that Boys Town could not spend more than $5 million a year. They decided that at least $100 million had to be piled up in an endowment.

The discovery of the Tax Reform Act of 1969, under which most nonprofit institutions and foundations are required to file form 990 with the Internal Revenue Service, provided the most important information. It revealed that at the end of 1970, Boys Home, Inc. was worth $191,401,421. The reporters estimated that by the end of 1971, its net worth was $209 million, rising at the annual rate of $17 million.

Next, a series of hard interviews took place. Alumni, attorneys of Boys Town, staff, the archbishop and monsignor who were at the top of the Boys Town "executives" and the 15 members of the board of directors were interviewed.

> We planned these interviews carefully. We actually scripted and rehearsed them—especially the one with the monsignor—

because we wanted to get on tape their "standard" responses to people who talked about Boys Town finances. Mick (the reporter) led the monsignor through about half an hour of friendly rambling before the priest became aware that the reporter was not just guessing. When Mick finally said we had a copy of Form 990, Wegner flared up; "That's confidential information!" Mick responded gently: "It's public record." The monsignor responded: "I know that, but it's still confidential!"

The story was headlined: "Boys Town—America's Wealthiest City?" There were 15 stories and 34 photos in all. One of the documents printed reproduced the Boys Town Christmas solicitation letter which begins "There will be no joyous Christmas season this year . . ." and opposite it ran Form 990 showing Boys Town's net worth and its annual income of $25.9 million.

Extensive administrative and internal changes have taken place at Boys Town since the story ran. Boys Town has also promised enormous sums to be used for institutes for treatment of speech and hearing defects in children and a national center for the study of child development. It is, however, financing these projects through new fund-raising letters.

"Have these stories produced long lasting change?" others ask. Yes—no doubt about it. The change is slower and less fundamental than I personally would like to see. I still fail to understand why the corporation's directors moved to resume the fund-raising appeals. But I also have faith in the basic concept: good reporting aids public understanding, which I believe has produced tempered but implacable pressure for reform.

The project still stands scrutiny as an example of the most important type of investigative reporting: the kind that simply tells an interested public how things work in our society. We did not allege any criminal acts. We were not writing about crime, but about institutional inertia. The people who ran Boys Town had been following an ancient institutional rule: if something is making money, leave it alone.

4

Filling in the Blanks:

Sources of Information to Develop the Story

"When something's gone wrong,
decent people find a way
to let the press know."

Somebody always knows.

That is the motto the tired reporter who has already hit a dozen deadends must keep repeating to himself. No matter what story is being pursued, somebody knows the circumstances and is capable of telling what he knows. He may have only part of the picture, but his pieces can be added to those picked up elsewhere. The Pulitzer Prize-winning story of Watergate, for example, was pulled together from thousands of fragments.

Many stories are literally on the record. Documents reveal what otherwise might remain secret. Generally, the investigative reporter prefers to go to the records first to build his case and then take it to the people involved for comment, confirmation or denial. And, reporters note, an additional benefit of records is that they don't change their minds and claim they were misquoted.

No matter what the approach, there are myriad places to obtain information. It's a matter of cultivating the human sources and being aware of the printed ones. In the next chapter, you'll learn how to handle the sources once you've located them. Here we're going to discuss examples of sources you'll want to consider contacting.

People

The Beat

An effective reporter doesn't merely check in with the people on his beat, he cultivates them. He stops by regularly and knows the people as individuals. He chats about children, duck hunting or high taxes. Gradually, defenses are lessened, and potential sources develop a sense of trust towards the reporter. Some investigative reporters say they banter with these people and show they value their opinions by listening, for example, to assessments of a presidential election or the need to send men into space.

When an investigative piece develops outside a beat, much of the direction comes from skillful handling of strangers in what is frequently a one-time interview. But for investigative pieces uncovered in the course of a beat, development depends very much on the nature of a reporter's pre-established relationship with these sources.

Whatever your beat, the best sources are often not the most obvious. Don't be a snob. Don't spend all your time with the head honcho, the one "in charge." Everyone who works in or around an office or governmental bureau knows some of what is happening. Talk to the state prisons director, but remember he has a secretary. She often knows as much as he does since she's seen the papers that passed over his desk. She may not have been in on the private chats, but, on the other hand, she may know more than he does about what's happening in other offices in the building. As go office gossip and intrigue, so go departmental policies.

Neither should your list of contacts include just the stereotyped dumb secretary who theoretically blurts out secrets. Quite often it's the smarter secretary who is the top source. "Secretaries are very helpful," says one reporter. "And they can be helpful without being disloyal." One may, for instance, give you information not on her boss but on other executives, because the tidbit makes her boss look good. And sometimes secretaries leak material at the boss's suggestion. "He doesn't want anybody to be able to pin it on him, but he wants you to know," says the reporter.

Similarly, middle-echelon personnel are often willing to talk. Get an organizational chart and seek them out because you might miss them otherwise. A nationally known editor and reporter says, "If you are dealing with large organizations, whether in the private sector or the government, some of your best sources are the second- and third-tier people. In the first place, many of them know more about what is going on than the top dog does. This is not unusual. Second, you are able to get a closer relationship. You can say to the second- or third-level guy, 'Come on, let's go across the street and have a drink.' You can get it on a social basis, whereas you are not going to be able to invite the vice president of the United States or the president of General Motors across the street for a drink. So these are always fertile sources, but ones which you have to approach with a considerable degree of caution: you have to remember that in all large organizations—armies, churches, businesses or governments—people down the line have an ax to grind and you have to learn when someone is giving you something or alleging something because they have the ax."

One reporter recalls a clerk he and a colleague located in a county courthouse. "We called him 'our man in the courthouse.' He was our man, by God. He spent just as much time working for us as he did for the county. He would call in every day. Just chat. We'd go have lunch with him, shoot the bull, not pumping him. But he knew we were interested. So he'd call in. Boy, it was amazing how much stuff he'd come across. From his point of view it was an ego trip. He worked in the clerk's office and had access to a lot of documents that came through, and having worked in there every day, he'd tie it all in. If a document came through, he'd be able to say, 'You know, that's funny. I remember something else on that.' And he'd call us, about someone buying land for a major shopping center or a politician showing up as new owner of a large tract."

In addition, doormen, janitors, cafeteria workers, telephone operators, chauffeurs, etc., all have bits of information. Naturally they won't be in on every story you seek. If the subject is nuclear power plants, you won't check with a janitor to get the lowdown. But there are stories which hinge on whether a person was in a building on a given night or on who's been visiting or on whether a phone call was placed. The night watchman, the doorman or the telephone operator may have the answer. The editor of a top-rated local paper recalls that he once broke a story on a big appointment because a waiter from a local hotel said the man in charge of making the decision had been seen lunching with a prospect who apparently was his final choice. In another instance, a radio reporter was trying valiantly but unsuccessfully to wedge himself into a jampacked executive mansion to cover a story. A mansion gardener the reporter had befriended earlier led him in a back way and left the other reporters swarming on the front lawn.

"What you find out," one political reporter says, "is there are a lot of people who love to tell reporters things. That's really true—if it's on somebody else. They just really get their kicks out of being knowledgeable and letting reporters know they are 'in'; that they, too, know things. Pretty soon, you find out there are some who just like to bull, so you've got to differentiate."

Or, as a former editor of a top New York daily puts it, "When something's wrong, decent people find a way to let the press know."

One caution: Don't spend too much time just chatting and kid yourself into thinking you're working. A singularly inept broadcast reporter in a state capital was infamous for reporting to the governor's office right after the 9 a.m. news, sitting down, sharing the coffee and talking about World War II while watching the aides work. He claimed that he was "cultivating sources," but he was actually wasting his day.

The Principal Figure

Although, as pointed out in the next chapter, it isn't wise to interview the main figure in a controversial case until you have definite information on the topic, it is important to contact him somewhere along the way. Never assume you know what he'll say or that he will refuse to talk to you.

Sometimes the principal figure is one of the best sources of a secret. Ego gets in the way, and he's compelled to let others know what clever or powerful or secret doings he's up to. On one occasion, for example, a massive fight in a state legislature over a tax bill had reached an impasse. A legislator closely identified with one side was literally smuggled into the governor's office while reporters were at the legislature covering other matters. But when the legislator returned to the statehouse and crowed, "Well, boys, I've just been to see the governor," he inadvertently also gave away the fact that the governor had agreed to his side's demands.

The same thing occurred in Washington, D.C., with a government official and two reporters. During the Cuban missile crisis, the official attended a luncheon and on leaving stopped to talk to two reporters about how "You just can't keep delicate negotiations out of the press." He told them he knew a big, big secret that the media would probably have within two days. The formerly unsuspecting reporters were tipped. By talking to other sources they discovered that Khrushchev, who had previously agreed to remove missiles from Cuba, had just caved in on the issue of removing certain bombers as well. After the story ran, the reporters heard from the astonished official: the story he had been thinking of was something minuscule. He had enticed them into battle, and they had brought back a victory larger than expected.

Off-Beat Sources

There are also numerous helpful people who are both off-beat and off your beat. Don't always depend on the regulars; that can lead to predictable, one-sided writing. Certain people keep up with things even though they're not newsmakers. You don't contact them for quotable material, but to find out if you are headed where you want to go. Woodward and Bernstein's "Deep Throat" is the most famous example. This type of source verifies or refutes what others have told you so you can determine whether to pursue that angle. Such "just-for-verification" sources exist in many areas. Quite often career bureaucrats can help you discern reality in the midst of a heated political battle. Or you might find a lawyer who can informally determine whether someone's acts are unethical or illegal. You might ask this source, "Can I run this by you to see whether I am right or wrong?"

Other sources off the beaten path include your own friends, your insurance agent, doctor, child's teacher. You might be doing articles in their fields. Their comments, like those of any source, must be weighed for the degree of self-serving material in them, but they are still handy for additional information or perhaps for initiating a story.

Other Reporters

One source frequently overlooked by beginners is the older reporter. This person has been on the scene for years and often can tell marvelous stories illuminating personalities on your beat or explaining how the state's higher education system was suddenly reorganized in a political swap or why it is that the lieutenant governor is supporting old Jones for the U. S. Senate. Shakespeare said in *The Tempest,* "The past is prologue." Nowhere is this truer than in reporting. And it doesn't occur just in politics. Why is that one school board member against building a new school? Why is a merchants' group opposing a shopping center? The older reporter can explain the past controversies and issues which leave their marks in today's events.

"Whenever the old hands in the statehouse pressroom asked me out for a beer, I always went," recalls one reporter. "I was delighted to pick up the flavor of state politics from the stories they swapped." Warmed by the beer and the convivial atmosphere, each of them was a fine raconteur, she recalls. "There was no way I, a novice, could lose."

Naturally, a reporter isn't going to come over and share his latest news item, but quite often even a competitor will give another reporter tips on why a committee *really* killed a bill yesterday. Some serious journalists care more about keeping the standards of the profession high than they do about making a newcomer work for every shred of news. The old tales about camaraderie in the police station pressrooms, where sober guys would write copy for their drunken friends from other newspapers, are at least partially true.

Another time to turn to fellow reporters is when you've been sent out of town on a story. If it's a story you alone are pursuing, go to the newspaper editors in the area and ask about potential contacts. They're usually helpful. The infinite value of well-developed sources is demonstrated by the fact that local reporters can quite often embarrass representatives of national papers and the networks who arrive to cover a prominent issue. The locals have sources to call on; the men and women new to the area quickly have to develop their own.

Moderation is the key here. Critics of the press, citing its supposed liberal East Coast bias, charge that reporters ask each other what they think and then, on that basis, report the news. Consider your colleagues as additional or beginning sources, never as ends in themselves.

In his now classic examination of the press, *The Boys on the Bus,* Timothy Crouse explored the pitfalls of pack journalism during the 1972 presidential campaign. His observations apply equally to any situation where a herd of journalists work in close proximity. Reporters who rely too heavily on the perceptions of their colleagues soon lose faith in their own judgment and become concerned not with what the story really is but with what their fellow journalists perceive as the story. Crouse believes that editors share in the blame for this common occurrence, but that it is a phenomenon of which all reporters should beware. He writes that while papers with large budgets realize prestige demands placing their own political reporters on the scene, for example, "they don't want reporters who are ballsy enough and different enough to make any kind of trouble. It would worry the shit out of them if their Washington reporter happened to come up with a page-one story that was different from what the other guys were getting. And the first Goddam thing that happens is they pick up the phone and call this guy and say, 'Hey, if this is such a hot story, how come AP or *The Washington Post* doesn't have it?' "

Such editorial attitudes, of course, are unlikely to encourage reporters to abandon easy, obvious developments and pursue a direction of their own. Investigative reporting, however, demands that they do so.

Social Functions

Social functions provide insights, even though they are not news themselves. Reporters may go to parties with legislators, for example, not only to strengthen a relationship but also to gauge the politician's character, to see who drinks with whom, who snipes at whom. Most reporters feel it is not ethical to quote anything they might hear while a source is in a relaxed, or perhaps inebriated, state. But most feel it's okay to later use other methods of pinning down a story idea that might have emerged in a casual conversation.

Law Enforcement Officers

It's not just the police reporter who keeps in touch with law enforcement. Many reporters, no matter what beat they have, try to maintain friends in the federal, state and local law enforcement agencies. A great many stories hinge on investigations—planned, completed or aborted—by one of these groups.

One investigative reporter, recalling his days on the police beat, tells how he approached law officers. His technique is valid for any reporter. "You've got to handle certain people very nicely. Like sheriffs and cops. I would talk to this one police chief for ten minutes. Not even ask him what happened. If I ever called him on the phone and said, 'Anything happening?' he would not tell a thing. So you talk to him a while, about what's going on, a little of this, of that, bemoan the course of events, the breakdown of society. And then say, 'By the way, did anyone get killed last night?'

"We got to the point with these guys that one time I got a call at home at 5 a.m. telling me to get down there, they had a big drug bust. They had promised to call if they ever had any stuff break during the night and they did."

As is discussed in a later chapter, law enforcement personnel must be approached with care, however. While they are useful to the reporter, they also tend to use the reporter for their own ends.

Peripheral Sources

In his haste to produce the story, a reporter might skip a type of source which can be crucial for a truly meaningful story. This source provides not information directly related to the case at hand, but rather provides background understanding, a feel for the factors which led to the main issues. For example, a *New York Times* piece on the celebrated murder trial of Joan Little, a black woman accused of killing the white jailer who she said had sexually assaulted her, covered all the principals in the situation but reached beyond these. The writer sought out not only people who might know what actually happened on the night of the incident, not only those who might have something to say which directly related to the question of guilt or innocence. He also interviewed numerous townspeople, many of whom knew nothing of the *cause célèbre* itself, but who could help him formulate conclusions about the environment which had produced this situation. Furthermore, he read books about the Southern experience in general, parts of which helped explain the broader implications of the central event.

Such sources, even if never quoted in the article, are invaluable for enabling the journalist to fully understand his subject. Someone writing a general piece about the attitude of college students toward cheating would, of course, interview numerous students on the subject. And the reporter composing an in-depth examination of why two particular students cheated would also need such interviews if he is to really understand the background of his protagonists.

Association Experts

No matter whether you're interested in the possible threats posed by tobacco or nuclear energy, cable TV or auto insurance laws, there is most likely an organization or association devoted to promoting or investigating that particular subject. Such associations, many of which are listed in the *Encyclopedia of Associations,* provide excellent, ever-ready sources. Both the staffs employed by these groups and the material they have are quite useful for the reporter.

It is vital, however, for the newsman to know the nature of the association with which he is dealing. Many associations are objective and provide data which can be trusted. In some states, for example, there are publicly financed institutions which research local and state laws and related governmental issues. A question on the tax rate in the state's 10 largest cities could thus be safely directed to one of their spokesmen. The Southern Regional Council in Atlanta, Georgia, is another such group. For years the council has collected statistics and in-depth profiles on numerous issues affecting that area. Reporters on the civil rights beat, for example, frequently used the council's figures on integration, knowing they were accurate.

Other types of associations, of course, are not so unbiased. Figures on integration obtained from either the National Association for the Advancement of Colored People or the White Citizens' Council could be treated as fact only if corroborated elsewhere. Yet spokesmen at these types of organizations are invaluable sources for questions of opinion, trends and movements. Similarly, many noncontroversial but biased associations such as chambers of commerce and medical groups often provide good lead material but should not be considered final sources of fact.

RECORDS

Thorough reporting includes awareness of how to find and use the printed record. Although the bureaucratic designation for a particular piece of information may vary from state to state, by and large the same kinds of facts are available everywhere.

"Do everything from records that you can, because the records will stand and they will be there when people run out on you," says one reporter. Recalling a series he did on corrupt election procedures, another reporter adds, "A guy can give you a sworn statement, but he can change it. Anyone who'll sell his vote can't be counted on to stick."

In our computer-minded society, endless records exist documenting our doings and misdoings. The problem lies in obtaining those records. *The Washington Post* was able to persuade an employee of a credit card company to reveal its files on a subject's hotel, restaurant and airplane ticket bills. From these emerged a clear picture of the man's movements.

Public Records

The public records in every state are valuable to the interested and patient investigator. Much of the material collected by government agencies "in the transaction of public business" is open to anyone who cares to look.

Although income tax records (except notices of delinquencies of federal taxes) are not generally available for perusal, tax records on property are. You can thus determine how much property a man owns in his own name, information which might be vital to prove or disprove many allegations. Another governmental office, sometimes called the Register of Deeds, can also tell you from whom he bought the property; how much he paid; when; and if any of the property has a lien attached. In addition, you can work backwards: start with the piece of land and find out who owns it. When a bit of spot zoning is passed to permit a shopping center to be built, it's convenient to be able to determine whether the zoning commission chairman owns the proposed site.

A man's marriages and his divorces, his driving record, criminal investigations or charges, whether (but not how) he voted in the last election, even his political affiliation, are all on record in most states.

All kinds of campaign expense records pertaining to staff salaries, purchases, contributions and loans are available, as are the filing forms themselves.

It's important to remember that the necessary facts may be on file but not in an obvious place. The knack is to keep looking in different places and to understand how to find a starting place. Every reporter should be familiar with the contents of his county courthouse. "You've got to know your way around the courthouse," says one young investigative reporter. "Court dockets, land records, things like that. You've got to be almost as knowledgeable as a real estate lawyer. Court records are the best because all that stuff is admitted under certain rules of evidence, sworn to and is just ideal. I could write stories from now until doomsday, working from civil court dockets on file."

Other Records

Telephone books; city directories listing street addresses, the names, spouses, and occupations of residents; "criss-cross" books which tell who has a certain phone number; records of credit bureaus and utilities; work permits, etc. The list is endless. Never assume a fact cannot be traced. Unless a business is a public utility, for example, its activities may appear to be a closed book, complete with lock and key. Yet, here too are sources on record. Check its annual stockholders report and the trade journals for that field. If pertinent, ask your boss to finance a Dun and Bradstreet report on its financial status. (And don't forget to track down a copy of the free "how-to" directions for reading a financial report, available from brokerage houses such as Merrill Lynch, Pierce, Fenner & Smith, Inc.).

Libraries

Several books, among them *Finding Facts* by William Rivers, are good reference tools for using the library as a source for story material.

Here, let us only call attention to two especially useful and less obvious library sources. The first are the government documents found in most libraries of any size. Covered in great detail in these reports are not only the workings of government but also general aspects of the subjects and issues on which governmental agencies concentrate. Woodward and Bernstein found General Accounting Office reports immensely helpful for understanding government expenditures and activities. More valuable to the reporter far from Washington, however, are the reports which Health, Education and Welfare, for instance, collects on its jurisdictional concerns, or those on housing compiled by the Department of Housing and Urban Development. Some government office somewhere may have pulled together statistics or information on any particular topic.

Using government documents isn't easy or speedy. But for a major story the work involved in uncovering material may well pay off. In addition, don't forget that local and state governments also collect material. Boards of election, for instance, compile stacks of figures useful in determining political trends.

Relatively new and useful lists of information found in the library are the source guides compiled by the *Columbia Journalism Review*. Mass transportation, occupational health and safety, land use, energy and reading a budget have all been CJR source guide subjects, for example. The source guides provide a comprehensive background bibliography and are invaluable for launching a reporter immediately in the right direction.

Don't forget other library sources such as the American Medical Association dictionary which gives a few pertinent facts about each doctor. Knowing when an M.D. graduated from med school and where he went, for example, might permit you to find a classmate who could provide background information on this doctor. Similarly, *Martindale-Hubbell* indexes lawyers, law firms and their corporate clients. It also provides an indication of just how financially successful an attorney is.

How to Find the Law, William R. Roalfe, ed., is another library source which will direct you to the statutes pertaining to particular situations.

Files

Building one's own files is a handy way to provide an in-house resource. It is imperative, of course, to maintain a file of one's own clips. In addition, keep a file of related material, carefully dated. For instance, if an education reporter is considering an in-depth report on the financial problems of private schools in his area, any and all articles, reports, wire copy, etc., concerning the general subject should be sought and saved. Even if his article spotlights only the local situation, examples and statistics on the broader story add scope and depth. Even one paragraph relating the local conditions to those across the nation can greatly increase a story's clout.

Personality files are another good bet. Quite often, quotes or positions from the individual's past can help develop a current story. Material on Senator XYZ's horse ranch which is not of value to today's piece may well be useful tomorrow when the senator decides to sponsor a bill on tax deductions for vet bills.

The trusting reporter may decide to skip his own filing and let the morgue do the job. He will discover the whimsey of this the first time he needs some clips. Materials vanish from the library, no matter how diligent the librarian. Except for very major publications and broadcasting facilities, budgets for the library staff are not large enough to insure that information on your specialty will be retained in full.

Freedom of Information Act

Reporters seeking source material need to be familiar with the Freedom of Information Act. The act outlines categories of material generated by the federal government that are public record. Under its provisions, officials refusing to supply such material are subject to punitive measures. News media members have no special rights under this law but are entitled to the same access as any other citizen. To file a request for information, reporters must have a reasonable description of the item being sought and must be willing to pay necessary fees.

For a detailed explanation of the act, write to the Reporters Committee for Freedom of the Press, 1750 Pennsylvania Ave., N.W., Washington, D.C. 20006. Ask for the guide, "How to Use the New 1974 FOI Act."

A CASE HISTORY ON SOURCE FINDING

In the following account, a reporter tells how he pulled together sources for a major story on the Ku Klux Klan in the days when Klan membership was a secret in order to heighten its image of terrorism. The aim of the story was to expose the leadership.

Note, 1) how the reporter overcame various impasses, 2) that the reporter refused to consider a telephone conversation sufficient documentation for a thorough story, 3) how he used records, 4) how common sense, intuition and luck meshed to enable him to locate his source.

"On information that had come to me from an informer, I

had the name of a man in a certain town who headed the local KKK unit and also held statewide Klan office. When I first got to the town, I tried to find this guy. And I couldn't. I began to suspect something was wrong. That's when I got the old city directories, because he wasn't listed in the current telephone directory nor the current city directory. Again he didn't show up. Obviously, he wasn't there, not in that city. I said, 'All right, I've got a bad name. I've been given either a bum steer or the guy was using an alias. Anyway, the name I had doesn't belong to anybody. He doesn't exist.' So then I started just hitting the pavement. I hadn't any contacts at all. Finally, I was referred to a man at the police department. 'Nah,' he said, he didn't know anything about it. 'Tell you who you ought to contact though,' he said. And it turned out it was an old cop who had sort of grown up with the town, an oldstyle cop on the beat who knew who his people were and who he had to police.

"This guy was at that time running a little Mom-and-Pop grocery store in one of the working class districts. I went to see him, and he was cagey. He wasn't sure he wanted to talk to me. But it was obvious he had some information. I didn't know how much he had, and how to evaluate it, but it was the only lead I had, so I figured it would be worth my while to take some time with him. And we chatted, and I let him warm up to me, and finally he said, yes, he did know a Klan leader. He had never heard of the name I had been given, but he did know who the leader really was. But he wouldn't tell me the name. So finally I said, 'Well, look, all I really need to do is talk to him. Could you set up a telephone interview?' He said, 'Well, maybe I could do that.' I left with the understanding that I would return the next day and we'd set up the interview.

"When I came back, he agreed to call him right there from his little store. Incidentally, it can be said without qualification at all that it is impossible to count the clicks on the telephone. That doesn't work. The phone was on the counter next to the cash register, and I couldn't see what he was dialing. I could see him dialing, but I couldn't see the digits.

"So he dialed and someone answered. He said, 'Hello, *John* D?' Well, it was later I connected all this, but he emphasized *John* D, not just John or John *D*. And in a few minutes he introduced me and I talked to the guy by phone. He identified himself. Yes, he was the head, the E.C., the Exalted Cyclops. I threw some questions at him to make sure he was, some things that nobody would know but him, but that I already knew from my other investigations.

"So we began talking and it was a pretty good conversation. He told only what he wanted told and he was full of braggadocio. He was tough, really tough. But it was a totally unsatisfactory interview because he controlled it, and the reporter always has to control the interview.

"During the conversation I kept hearing this damned train whistle, and it was from a switch engine, I knew that. And so my mind began to drift. One of the reasons the conversation was unsatisfactory was that I kept hearing the whistle. The store was in the woods on a hillside in an old mill neighborhood. But down at the bottom of the hill were the railroad tracks and they ran across the highway and along the other side. One minute I could hear the train out of one ear and the next minute I could hear it out of the ear on the phone—obviously going by the guy's house. So I knew he lived in that neighborhood. And I guessed he must live on the same side of the street. The train was closer to the store than it was to his house, but still I could hear it over the phone as it passed his house.

"I hung up and dashed back to the local newspaper office where I had borrowed a desk when I first came into town. I got out a city map and began working. Just plain old hard work, the unglamourous kind of work. I took the map and put down every house number there was in the neighborhood. After I had done that I drove down the street to make sure I'd gotten any new construction that might have been there. I counted houses on both sides of the street. I put down every damned house number; some of them didn't even have numbers. I knew that somewhere on a street near the store was the man I was looking for.

"I took the city directories and started filling in the map. I checked to see who lived in each house on the block, where they worked, how long they'd been there. I checked telephone numbers. I had my own master list of the name, address, employment, home ownership and phone of every house on the street.

"Then I fell back on this John D as opposed to any other. I remembered how he had stressed the name *John* D and I said, 'Maybe he has a cousin with the same last name and very similar first names.' I started another file. I took the last name of everybody on that half a mile of street and put it on a list and decided to work those names through the telephone directory. I took the first name, Adams or something, and worked it through the directory to see how many Adamses there were. Are there any Adams whose names are or could be John D and say, James D. And I worked my way down and, by God, I found it. You can't imagine the feeling I had when all of a sudden, bang, right there it was. It jumped out of the page at me. There was a John D. and a James D. with the same last name, on this street, and I've got John D's phone number.

"This had taken something like four days of hard work. I wanted to pick up the phone right then, and say, 'All right, you so-and-so, I've found you.' But no, I've got to go one step further; I am going to have the goods on him before I go back. So from the city directory I knew he worked for a shoe company. I found the personnel manager. Of course, they generally don't give out information on their employees. 'Why do you want it, anyway?' I told him, 'Well, I don't want to do your man a disservice. It's quite possible the one I'm looking for is a state officer in the KKK.' He said 'Oh man, you've got the wrong one. He's the last man for that.'

" 'Great,' I told him. 'In that case I really need to talk to him. But I might be able to eliminate him just by looking at his record.' The guy brought out the file, strictly on the q.t. When I looked at it, I knew I had the right guy. He had put down as a reference someone who also showed up on my earlier Klan list from the informer. I thought, 'I've got him.' But I played it real cool and thanked the personnel man and swore that his showing me the file would go no further.

"I dashed back to the newspaper office and called his

house. His wife answered and I asked to speak to *John* D. She said he was taking a shower. I told her, 'You tell him my name and that I'm the man he talked to on the phone yesterday.'

"I hung up and drove right to the house. She came to the door and called to him, 'It's the fella.'

"He said, 'Aw, hell, I'll see him.' "

5

Drafting the Battle Plan:
Controlling the Interview

*"You don't go in and say,
'Did you steal the money?' "*

How a reporter approaches his sources determines what kind of story he develops; indeed, his approach is crucial to whether he gets a story at all. A severe misstep can cost him the story as well as several weeks or months of effort. It is disappointing to have a story come to naught for any reason, but to have it shot to pieces because of the reporter's own error is a frustration ulcer-prone journalists should avoid.

The newsman must maintain control—of himself, of the individual interviews and of the investigation as a whole. Once a reporter loses his grasp on any of the three, he is forced into a most uncomfortable defensive position.

SELF-CONTROL

Preconception and Fairness

Before beginning research, much less prior to deciding the story angle, the reporter must be certain that he is open-minded enough to follow the investigation wherever it leads. Investigative reporter Lincoln Steffens long ago advised: "Clear your mind of all pre-possessions, then go to the enemies and the friends of your subject. Take all that they give you of charges, denials and boasting; see the man himself; listen sympathetically to his own story; and, to reduce to consistency the jumble of contradictions thus obtained, follow his career from birth through all its scenes, past all the eyewitnesses and documents to the probable truth.''

The consequences of being emotionally involved in a story can be perilous. "It enables the guy to come back and say, 'Aw, that reporter was all involved in this thing, and he couldn't see the truth. I couldn't talk to him. He was just ranting at me.' This hurts you, because you, the reporter, become the issue. You don't want to ever become part of things if you can avoid it," says one reporter. Reflecting on their early work, reporters often say that they bore a "missionary zeal," desiring to see changes as a result of their stories. They were outraged by the conditions they perceived and set out to "get" somebody.

But, warns a veteran, "Even though many times, I have thought 'Oh, you S.O.B., I am going to nail your ass now,' after I've nailed him there is a letdown and I realize he is just another human being. I make mistakes. If he ever tried to nail me, he probably could. And every time you get a little less of that 'vengeance is mine.' You get an elation when you've done a job well, but the elation comes from having done the job rather than from a real kick at having nailed somebody.

"I think the mark of a mature reporter is when he can do his job because he knows it has to be done," the reporter continues, "and not feel that personal vengeance is a satisfaction. I don't really get any pleasure out of killing a man's career."

One editor says he prefers that his staff be a bit sorry for their subjects so he knows they are not forming a lynching party. "If there is any weakness in our business, it's our glee at other people's troubles," he says.

It must also be noted that a "give-'em-hell" attitude is conducive to making serious errors. An investigative reporter who's positive he possesses 100 per cent of the truth on every issue may distort the facts to justify the emotional stance he has taken.

Maintaining an objective stance is necessary not only when the reporter dislikes his subject. The same nonpartisan position should be evidenced when interviewing a person you admire about a topic you support. Just as you don't argue with someone whose position you oppose, neither do you use the interview to applaud someone whose cause you favor. In the story, the facts can speak for themselves. This does not mean that you should be cold or unsympathetic to the interviewee's circumstances. Indeed, some very successful investigative reporters advocate a strong display of understanding for the subject's field and problems. Just remember not to use the interview as a forum to promote your own opinions.

In a memo to a reporter, one editor warns against letting feelings govern an interview. "It seems to me," he writes, "that the really successful reporters appear to be the most neutral in conveying their personal feelings. They're like psychiatrists are supposed to be—they just say um-hum and move on to the next question. Just as the reporter must not place himself in a story, he must not thrust himself into the conversation beyond asking the necessary questions. Reporters just don't count. Newspapers don't count. They're inert. They're conductors, not currents. The action, the identity, the ego trip belong to the sources and the protagonists, not the reporters—at least that's the way the public must perceive it, and that's the way sources would like to have it. In fact, probably the most successful reporters seem to be those who have just no feelings at all."

Demeanor

Self-control is not exemplified by abrasiveness or rudeness. In an attempt to show they are in command, some reporters go to great lengths in their ferocity. While such tactics may satisfy the ego, the newsman will soon learn that they work only once. People don't respond to brusque treatment, not even when the people themselves are in the wrong. If the reporter has the facts on his side, he should not have to resort to histrionics or browbeating.

"I think maybe Hollywood has done us a disservice because too many people still come into the business thinking that

the way to function as a reporter is to be tough, really tough,''
one investigative reporter believes. "And that is so wrong. Yes,
you have to have the ability to be tough. You have to know
when to go for the jugular, but also when to lay off it. I think
you could probably justify the existence of a charm school for
reporters. You should always be polite. Always. You are so
damned unctuous sometimes you just ooze politeness. You
never, never go in to interview anyone with a chip on your
shoulder. Never. I don't care how big the other man's chip is;
you're just as obsequious as you can be. That's the way to get
information.''

Another reporter adds, "I like to be as unabrasive as possible. I like to move in on someone's blind side, get the news
without them being aware I'm getting it. Some reporters today
say, 'Hell, if they don't like us, they don't have to read our
paper.' I don't think the reporter should kowtow to anyone, but
you don't have to make an ass out of yourself getting a story.''

Being perceived as a pleasant, albeit hard-eyed, person
pays dividends. "A good investigative reporter is one who, no
matter who he screws, did it fairly; he isn't just out to get someone. The best ones, no matter what they've found and written,
are still liked. They can maintain their standing because they
can project a toughness, persistence and perserverance without
being so abrasive people just collapse,'' says another journalist.

It's also considerably easier to ask questions about matters
you don't understand or are unfamiliar with if your initial approach has been smooth. A reporter may think he has all his information and needs only to confront the major figure to wrap
up his story, but then that interviewee may add new information
that alters earlier conclusions. How much easier it is to digest
the additional material and ask meaningful questions if the interview has been unemotional. Even if the man you're talking to
threatens or tries to sock you, resist the impulse to return his
blows.

Developing a successful demeanor may be role-playing,
but much of reporting is just that, with the reporter slipping into
the attitude and approach required by the problem. "In order to
get the best out of the interview,'' says one experienced news-

woman, "I definitely find myself talking to a corporation president in a manner different from that in which I hail a coastal fisherman who's helping me with a story on the menhaden run." Such changes are not devious; all of us do this in our daily lives. We reveal a different character to our spouses than we do to our bosses. Our movements, our facial expressions, the tone and volume of our voices vary according to the situation. Reporters just adopt these roles for a professional end.

One final note on demeanor: the use of sex appeal is a common, if questionable, practice. Many male reporters quite consciously shower secretaries with extra attention and flattery, which is fine if both parties understand the game. Although this line of approach is blocked to female journalists, they work their wiles on male contacts. Even though sex appeal won't really help a reporter who is, after all, a witless dummy, it's an extra bit of ammunition used by many. Be careful, however, in how far you take a playful relationship. Difficulties arise when the other person considers your overtures serious.

Controlling the Interview

Getting In to Talk

It's amazing how few reluctant sources there are. Most people make the journalist's job much easier because they love to gossip and tattle. A telephone call is all that is necessary to set up most interviews. "Few people can keep a secret; that's the nature of the beast," says one former reporter-turned-editor.

Yet major stories sometimes involve people who are hesitant to talk. Even if they themselves are innocent of any error, they may be wary of being interviewed. Afraid of being misquoted, sued or losing their jobs, they may decline to talk. Just the prospect of appearing in print or on television scares many people. And when the subject has something to hide, the difficulty of obtaining access is further complicated.

The investigative reporter's task is to overcome these obstacles to uncover the story. Persistence is the first factor. Bernstein and Woodward, for example, pursued one unwilling source with 28 visits and calls before they got the information they wanted. If your phone request for an interview is denied, try to keep the subject on the line chatting about anything—shift to a neutral topic and keep talking. Perhaps he will warm up. Or call him back and jump in with "I really do need your help, and I'm sorry we didn't get a chance to talk before, and I thought it was so important to me I would like to ask you again if I could come over to talk with you."

Sometimes the desired subject refuses even to come to the phone if he knows reporters are trying to reach him. In this case, some newsmen call and ask for "Joe" rather than "Mr. Smith," hoping to give the impression that a friend is on the line.

In some instances, where you know that the subject will immediately hang up as soon as he finds out who's calling, don't phone. Just walk into his office, or catch him outside his home. People have a much more difficult time being nasty in a direct confrontation. If the closed-door treatment is likely, some reporters claim they walk right by a man's secretary, say "Good morning" and casually saunter into the inner office. Others camp on his doorstep until he emerges and then try to persuade him to talk.

Once your subject is actually present, keep your foot in the door. In *All the President's Men,* a persuasion sequence went like this: Reporter knocks on door, is refused entry, asks for cigarette so he can get in. Sympathizes. Asks if he can sit down and finish cigarette. Sister of subject offers coffee. He sips very slowly. Plays with dog. Asks only casual, sidestepping questions. Finally talks of initials, not names, to ease the interviewee's sense of actually telling secrets.

Another technique basic to persuading a bashful source to talk is to stress how the interview will help the source himself. Tell him how revealing the truth will insure that others understand and forgive what happened. Try to make him see how explanations are often less damaging than insinuations arising from incomplete knowledge. If he is not personally involved in wrongdoing, appeal to his sense of honesty and desire to disassociate himself from the problem.

"Accidently" bumping into the man you want to question

is a good way to gather information without arousing suspicion. If you make a point of setting up an appointment, your subject may become worried and withdraw. But if you find out where he's likely to be on a certain day and just happen by, a "Good morning, how are you?" can easily turn into a "By the way, what about so-and-so?" This works best, of course, on people with whom you are already acquainted.

A final way to reach a reluctant source is to "launder" your call. Get someone else to ask your questions for you, someone to whom the source is likely to talk. Even though such secondhand information cannot be directly attributed, it may still corroborate another source or suggest a possible alternate approach.

Broadcast newspeople face a double challenge in trying to persuade a hesitant individual to be interviewed. First, the subject must be coaxed into talking, and then he must be cajoled into talking with a microphone under his nose. It's easy to tell someone, "Forget about the camera," but as the nervousness of the beginning newsman himself attests, that is next to impossible. Reporters can offer reassurance by pointing out that even network broadcasters sometimes make fluffs on the air and that these slips make the interview more natural. They also tell people that it's the content of what they say, not the elocution, in which listeners are interested.

Identifying Yourself as a Reporter

Another aspect of the interview concerns the proper method and time at which the reporter should announce that he is a representative of such-and-such news organization. In one type of story, that in which the reporter questions the subject directly, intending to quote him by name, it is only fair that the subject know exactly with whom he is dealing. Yet the reporter standing in the midst of a riot is not obliged to use a bullhorn to inform bystanders that he is present.

Similarly, for mood pieces on topics like poverty in Appalachia or the President's popularity, most reporters think it acceptable to chat naturally with people they encounter without immediately identifying themselves as journalists. But when the more personal questions such as "How much do you earn in a year?" or "Have you ever been on food stamps?" arise, it's necessary for the answerer to know he is revealing such facts to a reporter who might use them publicly. It's possible to just shift gears calmly by saying, "Well, I'm a reporter with ———, and I'm doing a series on this. I'd like to talk further with you about it." If rapport has been developed, such a comment won't be offensive or send your source scuttling away.

There is a third type of story in which identification is not necessary and can kill the article before it gets started: the exposé of what an open-to-the-public organization or business is doing. This kind of story involves, for example, a reporter comparing various estimates for repairing a broken television set; sending youngsters to X-rated films to check the theatres' admittance policies; or posing as a mental patient. Since in these cases you are determining the response the public normally receives, it is fair to represent yourself only as an individual. Before you wrote your story, of course, you would return to each subject and ask for comment on what you found out.

Beginning the Interview

The quickest way to scare your subject is to acknowledge the significance of what he's telling you. The tone and pace of the interview, therefore, usually must underplay any excitement you feel at its revelations. Normally when requesting an interview, the reporter gives only a general idea of the topic in which he's interested. There are very few people who, when getting your call, won't ask what you want to talk about. Your answer, in touchy cases, is as vague as possible. If you want to talk to a politician about possible illegal campaign practices, you tell him the subject is "Oh, campaign stuff," or "campaign finances." You don't say, "Well, I think your finance director pocketed every second dollar you took in." In the same vein, when you arrive and begin to talk, your first questions are the easy ones: How many people were on your staff? How many helped with speech writing? How many secretaries? You lead gradually to the real subject: finances and the staff responsible for those decisions.

"You don't go in and say, 'Did you steal the money?' " says one reporter. "You keep building on the little admissions. Suddenly the fellow realizes he's admitted 75 per cent of it, and when you ask him the big one, he figures that he's told you all the rest so he might as well go all the way."

Under very few circumstances, if any, will you tell the interviewee the questions ahead of time. Presidents of the United States sometimes demand and receive this privilege; refuse it to almost everybody else. Broadcast reporters frequently encounter people who ask that this be done. There are numerous objections to granting these requests. First, rehearsing the questions destroys spontaneity, removing the distinctiveness with which people naturally express themselves. The interviewee who rehearses his answer with you will not repeat his reply when the camera starts rolling. He knows you've heard it before, so he rephrases it and it's never as colorful or artless as the original. And, if the interview is on a controversial topic, the person has had precious minutes to formulate a statement which becomes more a defense than an answer. Further, for both broadcast and print reporters, offering questions in advance removes the opportunity to pursue issues which rise unexpectedly or to follow up unsatisfactory replies.

Asking the Questions

The way in which you ask questions often determines the usefulness of the answers you receive. Questioning is critical. You should have your questions and the order in which to ask them decided in advance.

"The main thing is not to put your subject offguard initially," says one investigative reporter. "I am a gregarious person anyway and am sort of loose. They sort of figure 'Who is this kid, why should I worry about him?' And so I play it like that, like I don't really know what I'm doing, so that it's no sweat. But what you have to do is not allow their minds to get on the track. It is possible for the interviewee, hearing the direction of your questions, to figure out what you are going to ask next. So I take it in an illogical sequence. Sometimes I ask follow-up questions, of course, but I am weaving all around.

After I've led them all over the field I come back in with the critical question, the bombshell, so they don't have time to figure out in advance what their best response is. I like to go into interviews and know every answer that the guy is going to give in advance. You should ask questions so that you know what the answers are and throw in a couple to test their truthfulness. I also let them know I know their answer is correct, which disarms them.''

The old "Have you stopped beating your wife" approach is valid. The reporter asks not "Did you —?" but "Why did you —?" or "How did you —?" Otherwise, the subject can simply answer, "No, I did not," leaving the reporter with a blank notebook and nowhere to go. In one article written during the Watergate period, a newsman was trying to ascertain if some state officials had bought watches with concealed tape recorders and other bugging equipment. "We didn't go in and say, 'Did you buy those things?' " he recalls. "We asked 'Have you disposed of those tape recorders you bought?' You give the impression you know an awful lot more than you do, and this scares people to death. Chances are the guy will unload to some extent unless he's a very cool, tough and cagey customer. Then there's nothing you can do except keep throwing it out to him and see if he'll take the bait.''

Again, casualness is best. Don't say, "Tell me about that terrible prison riot"; rather suggest to the official that "I heard that you had some trouble out at the prison this morning," and lead into the underlying causes of the disturbance.

The following story from a newspaper editor in a major university town illustrates how phrasing the question makes the difference. Believing that he had the name of the man already selected to be the new chancellor, the editor called the public information office at the campus where the man was currently employed. "I said, 'Look, we understand they want to make this announcement simultaneously, and the university news bureau here is ready to go. When will you be ready to go with the announcement up there?' And the fellow was shocked and he said, 'We haven't made the decision yet. We're waiting for the president to get back and it will be decided then.' Of course that was all we needed to know we did have the right name. We just threw a little curve at somebody.''

Throwing a little curve is what most reporters delight in. One curve involves bluffing strictly on the basis of a hunch. Such a device requires the projection of strong self-confidence.

For a story concerning an ex-convict's charge that he had bribed an official to parole him, an investigative reporter got the facts strictly on the strength of a bluff. Repeated attempts to document the man's accusation had failed; the reporter decided to confront the official directly. "Knowing this guy, I just figured that to blast anything out of him, I would have to hit him with it head on.'' Violating his own basic rule of the soft approach, the reporter "sat right by his desk with my notebook in hand. I opened it up and said, 'Chuck, tell me about this damned case and don't tell me any damned lies.' He said, 'What do you want to know?' I said, 'The whole story.' And he told me. If he had said, 'No comment,' I would have been dead. But he started to talk and kept telling me things. Every once in a while he would reach a place, look up and see if I was satisfied. I wouldn't say anything. I would just look at him and then he'd start to talk again. He laid out the bare bones so that I could document the story elsewhere. And after he had talked for a considerable length of time, I knew enough to ask intelligent questions. I asked them as if I had known the answers all along. When I left, the story was made except for picking up the documents.''

Some reporters admit that they torpedo a subject by telling him a horrible story they've supposedly heard. In order to convince this reporter of the falseness of the story, the subject will admit the truth in full detail. This is, of course, dishonest, and many journalists do not favor such a practice. Some, while disavowing it as a general procedure, say that the importance of the issue determines whether the method is justified.

When the interview reaches its central topic, the questions should be short and delivered one at a time. Remember the technique used by cross-examiners: each query is on a direct point, and each leads to the next. Try to make the source answer important questions specifically and repeat his answers in varying contexts. If possible, let the source mention the key aspect without prodding.

Listening to the Answers

An interviewer must not be so concerned with his questions that he doesn't fully hear the replies. Listen and listen well. An attentive ear can catch nuances which may need clarification. Let your source talk. Encourage him by "active" listening, by nods and murmurs, rather than by a constant barrage of questions. Don't interrupt to offer your opinion on the topic, tempting as it may be to share your own expertise.

Unanswered points can slide by the interviewer who's not really paying attention and for a broadcast reporter, it's often impossible to get another interview. Deadlines may preclude a second filming, or the subject's refusal or budget considerations may make a retake impossible. Even for the newspaper reporter, having to call back and ask questions that should have been included initially, questions that quite possibly will be answered differently after time has elapsed, is embarrassing.

Some reporters are known for their ability to "listen" a subject into confession. One famous woman journalist is supposedly so shy that her interviewees, unsure of what to do with all that silence, simply blurt out things they think she wants to know. There is also a possibly apocryphal story of a political reporter who got answers from the governor by simply sitting and staring at him across his desk. The governor would finally relent and start talking. Television reporters can simply ask a question, listen to the incomplete answer and let the camera keep running. The dead silence except for the whirr of the camera will often make the subject so uncomfortable he will resume his conversation and divulge more than he had intended. Conversely, conspicuously cutting off the camera or closing the notebook may indicate to the person being interviewed that you're aware he isn't telling you anything. He may then sheepishly advance to more solid ground.

Listening well also enables a good reporter to catch suspicious answers or honest errors. Some phrases may be tipoffs that the response is a deliberate evasion. "Not to my direct knowledge,'' or ''I don't personally know about that,'' or ''No, I don't recall an *October* meeting where that occurred,'' are all clues that the question had best be asked again in a different way.

One reporter says he devised the ''Two-minute Mile Rule'' to catch potential errors. ''A source in the Justice Department gave me the date of a payment to a government witness in a trial. The date preceded the trial. I asked him if that was correct, and he said that's what the records showed. Actually it was wrong in the records, because if a witness is paid beforehand that can be construed as a direct bribe. If he is paid afterwards supposedly that is all right, just as they wave lesser prison terms and stuff in front of witnesses. I should have applied my 'Two-minute Mile Rule' and then I would have realized the record was wrong. Under this rule, if someone tells me the mile was just run in two minutes, I don't put that in the paper straightaway because it is so unbelievable it is probably not true. You've got to check a statement like that out in every possible way because it is so critical and there are common sense reasons to doubt it.''

Handling the Liar

It is not infrequent that the investigative reporter encounters a person who is plainly lying. Skepticism should, therefore, be an inherent part of reporting. ''I ask myself,'' says a veteran, '' 'What's his motive for telling me this? What's his pitch? What are his connections?' He invariably wishes someone ill; the person you are concentrating on is no friend of his, and he means to put the screws on him through you. This can color much of what he tells you, or leaves out.'' Guilty until proven innocent is, unfortunately, the safest approach to follow. Take nothing at face value.

On one-time investigative pieces, when a reporter feels a subject is lying, he must remain cool and in control. A professional can't lunge across the desk and throttle the liar with his own necktie. He can't even tell the man that his lies are obvious, for a confrontation won't result in a story. Most reporters handle a dishonest answer by turning it back on the subject.

They take down the untruths, ask additional questions and let the person dig himself in deeper, forcing him into more and more obvious lies until finally he says something which can be proved otherwise. To handle a subject more gently, the reporter can say, "Well, Mr. So-and-so, I'm sure you feel you're right, and I wouldn't want to dispute you, but what about this?" or "Are you aware that Mr. Jones said such-and-such?" or "I'm confused. There's a document in the courthouse which seems to indicate . . ." Go slowly. If the person being interviewed has a chance to change his mind and save face once he realizes lies won't work, quite often he will do so. And while expressing your moral indignation may be satisfying, getting the story is better.

Some reporters, however, when being dodged or lied to by people on their regular beats, are more direct in their comments. "Certain people I can accuse of lying," says one political reporter. "After awhile they hate you so much you get along with them really well. This one state official I know well enough to say 'You know, George, I don't believe a damned word you're saying.' But you really don't get anywhere doing that with people on a regular basis. You've got to figure this: if someone's going to get reamed in the paper you can't say anything to give them something to come back at you with. If it's someone you don't know well or don't have a good relationship with, if you accuse him directly of lying, he can say, 'This reporter had his mind made up before he asked me anything.' "

Knowing the reasons people lie to reporters helps us understand how to deal with the liars. It is somewhat insulting for the journalist when his subject lies, because it makes the newsman feel as if he appears gullible. More likely the man knows he may get caught, but feels that will come later. Right now he just wants this particular reporter off his neck so he can have time to think. He buys time by lying. Occasionally someone lies to inflate his own position or because he thinks the truth will be misunderstood. This can confuse things for a reporter who assumes there are always sinister reasons for falsehoods.

During a political campaign, for example, a reporter asked a candidate's treasurer for names of contributors. Thinking the list of people was not impressive enough, the treasurer added some possibilities who in fact had not yet contributed. The reporter could have run the story and made the candidate look bad. However, when the reporter learned that the treasurer had not lied because of campaign shenanigans but because of his own ego, the reporter killed the story. Ironically, one of the contributors who denied giving money had actually done so. He was a wealthy but politically naive farmer who was so frightened by the newsman's call that he felt he must have done something wrong because a reporter was asking him questions.

One last word about lying: when a reporter finds himself with multiple interpretations of the facts and no idea whom to believe, there are several points to remember. First, it is not always incumbent upon the reporter to declare before God and man who is telling the truth. It is sufficient to cite the various interpretations and let the public decide for itself. Second, there are not two sides to every issue. Instead, there are far more, sometimes a side for every person involved. And third, although everyone in a controversy may be telling a different version of what happened, they may all believe they are relating the truth. Their perceptions of the facts are simply different. People may dispute without lying.

Keeping the Mike

Television and radio reporters have a special problem pertaining to interview control—hanging on to the microphone. Whether it's a desire to ham it up or merely the need to keep his hands busy, an interviewee may insist on grappling for the mike. Don't let him do so. First, having the mike gives him control of the interview. One way a television reporter indicates the first answer has been sufficient and that it's time for the second question is by tilting the hand mike back towards himself. If the subject is holding the mike, this is impossible. He rattles on until he's ready to *let* you ask another question. An amusing but distracting battle develops as the reporter and subject try to wrest the mike from each other. The interviewee may actually clamp his hand over the reporter's, but the newsman must tighten his grip and hang on. The subject will, in a few seconds, feel uncomfortable at holding hands with the reporter and will drop his arm. If he tries again and fails, he will understand that he is there to answer questions, but that you are calling the shots.

When to Go "Off the Record"

Sometimes people are willing to talk but insist that it be "off the record." Generally this is not what they mean. Since this is the only term they know, they use it when actually they mean you can use the information but may not reveal that it came from them. To reporters "off the record" means not for use. Period. Thus it is vital to clarify with the potential source what stand he is actually taking.

Off-the-record material poses special problems for reporters which we will discuss in a moment. For now it is important that we distinguish terms commonly used by journalists in order to reach an understanding with sources about how material is to be attributed.

On the Record. This means that anything from the conversation may be used in part or full and clearly attributed to the person involved. There are no limitations on usage. Obviously the reporter seeks as much on-the-record material as possible.

For Attribution but not for Direct Quotation. Whenever someone is dealing with a controversial subject, he may be willing to comment but not wish to be bound by any exact phrases. Therefore, he will permit you to quote him but only in paraphrase, not in direct quotations.

Not for Attribution. Here the reporter may use the material but only in such a way that it is not connected with the person who provided it. The reporter thus takes the responsibility for the validity of the subject matter; the provider of the information has the satisfaction of seeing it released without any danger to himself. Journalists, therefore, must be careful that they are not fed a line which they then innocently repeat.

Off the Record. This term means exactly what it says. After an off-the-record session none of the information, no leads arising from that information or any suggestion of it is to appear. The person skilled in dealing with the media sometimes uses "off-the-record" comments to manipulate the situation.

"People go off the record," says one reporter, "because they want to control the interview, and if you go off the record because they want to, you are playing their game, and I don't want to play their game. Politicians are worst on this; and it is pernicious because they corrupt newspaper reporters. I'll guarantee you if you pick out any good experienced political reporter that man knows a heck of a lot more than he's ever printed. And after a while it is cumulative. It builds up where he's a storehouse of knowledge he can't get into print. And the stuff he writes is just blah. The youngster who is hungry, especially in politics, can just cut out these oldsters who are trying to protect their sources."

Another reporter advises against accepting off-the-record material for a similar reason: "Sometimes you get trapped by having good material on this basis. Of course, if someone talks and talks, and then says, 'Oh, of course, all that I have said this afternoon is off the record,' that isn't the way the game is played, and I have told people who've tried it exactly that. None of this retroactive stuff.

"I have been in the position of getting something off the record and later having a chance to get it on the record. Also, I have gotten stories off the record which I had only from one source, but later learned a competitor was working on the same story. Then I've gone back to the guy who gave it to me and said, 'Look, I know I got this from you off the record, but I know they are going to print it tomorrow. What I am asking is to release me from the pledge so that I don't sit there and get a kicking.' Most of the time if he knows you are telling the truth and it's going to get out anyway, he'll let you go ahead and run it.

"When I get something from one person off the record and then pick up the same thing from another place, I don't think I've ever failed to call the first person and say, 'I am not violating your confidence; I could have picked this up anyway, and if So-and-So told me, he's probably telling other people. I want you to know we are going with it,' " he continues. "It's important to get back to that initial source just to keep my dealings with him straight. If he still says not to release the information I am not bound by this. I have at least tried to make him know I am not breaking a confidence."

Background and Deep Background. Often government sources will provide "background" sessions which are off the record. Thus, in these cozy little chats the source will explain to the reporter the background of some news event. The budget this year is so high, a city official will note, because the mayor and a councilman refused to compromise and insisted on including all their pet projects. Now the reporter understands the background of the budget, true, but he cannot report it because he agreed to go "on background." Background situations are, therefore, normally unproductive unless they are only temporarily off the record and considered reportable at a future date.

When a source is on "deep background," he does not independently provide information but merely explains, expands or modifies material the reporter has already collected. Again there is no direct use of his offerings and certainly no hint of any kind as to his identity is ever released. Like background sources, deep background sources help the reporter grasp the extent and meaning of the situation.

CONTROLLING THE SITUATION

The direction from which sources are worked depends on the story itself and the reporter's prior relationship, if any, with the sources. If the investigative piece is about the effects of unemployment or the pace of inflation, for example, then the sequence for contacting sources would be determined only by common sense.

However, if the article involves "getting the goods" on someone or putting together a puzzle, sequence is vital. In some stories, even if all your sources knew you were coming and knew whom you had contacted, their answers would still be the same. In cases where people are trying to keep a secret under wraps, as soon as one source gets a call from a reporter, he will telephone all other parties so that their versions of what happened will mesh. Everyone will become purveyors of a doctored tale. "I was tracing some money in a political campaign," says one reporter, "and I asked this man about it. He told me that this certain guy gave the money. I didn't know him and asked how to get in touch with him. 'Oh, don't worry, I'll have him call you,' my source said. And he did. But by the time he called they had gotten the story lined up." In this instance the reporter could have prompted the source to make the phone call while he waited, or else gotten the phone number from him and immediately placed the call himself. The point is to lessen the possibility that story sources have time to cover themselves.

If you start with the least important people, those on the periphery, and with the records, by the time the subject of your article gets suspicious you will have enough material to understand what has occurred. Reveal as little as possible of what you are after when talking to sources; keep calm; don't accuse anybody of anything. Just ask each individual the questions to which he might have firsthand answers.

"Once I get the tip, I call the outsiders first. You don't go to that guy in the middle," warns a reporter. "Don't go to the one you are going to stick it to. Because you've got to know the law. If there are documents, get the documents. See what the documents say because sometimes you'll get your target and in the interview he will give you a story that sounds plausible. But then when you read the documents afterwards, they contradict him. Then you gotta go back to him. So don't go in until you are ready to pop him, documents and all. Have it all laid out."

If you must approach the principal figure first because no one else can give you even a hint of the answer, be careful that his explanation doesn't keep you from looking further. Even though he has admitted nothing, his denial may provide the clue you need to start in another direction. For instance, if you ask him whether he met with the governor to discuss a highway contract and he says, "The governor and I haven't discussed anything like that," then the key may be in his use of the phrase, "the governor," leading you to suspect that instead he spoke with a top gubernatorial aide.

As the reporter moves from interview to interview, the

story should begin to take shape. One source will blend into another, suggest further contacts, additional reading material. In the beginning all a reporter can do is stake out a general line of inquiry, staying free to shift when something else turns up. The necessity of hanging loose cannot be stressed too often, for an open mind is mandatory.

In some instances, you are finally able to get some information out of a person but can't use it without getting him into trouble because only he and one other person know the secret. If he tells, it will be readily apparent who did so. However, if three or more people are in on something, you stand a much better chance to work it out because no one will know for sure who told.

If the matter being investigated is political corruption, you've got state or local political people involved, either calling for investigations or bringing someone to trial. Parochial political interests often make local officials reluctant to take such actions, especially if that state has elected judges and prosecutors, because they run on the same ticket with the people involved.

If it's election fraud involving the "in" party, it will be difficult to break out the story. In these instances, you might want to consider involving the federal government; literally making a "federal case" out of it. If you can strike a deal, the federal officials get the information you've dug up, and when and if they crack the case, your news organization gets the jump. You must decide, on the basis of the material you've found, whether a "federal case" could make the difference in getting laws tightened, a crook sent to jail or some bad situation corrected.

Federal agents have access to income tax records and can obtain bank records which state and local investigators can't. If you're trying to follow the dollar in a story, and you get hung up because you can't get at the information, federal officials might make the difference in your having to toss all your spadework into a file drawer and forgetting it or eventually getting something you can write about. This method is applicable in only certain investigative pieces and it's a good idea to know the federal officials you're dealing with, such as the federal district attorney, FBI agents or area IRS supervisors. The dangers of working with government officials cannot be overlooked, however. They are discussed in Chapter 7.

A CASE HISTORY ON
CONTROLLING THE SITUATION

Several years ago, a reporter initiated an investigation that involved one political leader, two "wives," two states and an enormous amount of work from records. As you read the following account, note: 1) how initial tips came from varied sources, 2) how the newsman who first heard of the possible story almost blew it, 3) how the investigation as a whole was plotted so that it worked down to the center in ever-tightening circles, and 4) how the final interviews were staged to prevent collusion. The story is told by the reporter who ran the investigation.

"A national news magazine did a roundup on emerging Republican leaders in the South and ran the story with photos. Among the people included was Tom Smith (not his real name), chairman of the State Republican Party, who was also a candidate for the state senate.

"Just after the issue came out, a Roanoke, Virginia, political reporter was at church, when a woman parishioner came up to him and said, 'You know, they showed a man in a magazine the other day who looks a lot like one of my neighbors named Smith. They are the spit and image of one another.' This reporter then called us in our state and said he wanted to do a funny piece on how the men look alike. I thought about it for a minute and told him not to do anything until I could get to Roanoke. I pulled our files on Smith and within the hour I was on a plane to Roanoke.

"After discussing the situation, reflecting on Smith and his charm, suavity and such, we thought we might have a story. The man in Roanoke was known as W. Thomas Smith, had a wife and two children. The one in our state was William T. Smith and had a wife and a son. How to check it out?

"First we sent a photographer to Smith's Roanoke house to take a picture of the car in the driveway. It had Virginia plates and was, can you believe it, a black Edsel. You know, the loser? The registration turned out to be in the name of Smith's company in his home in our state. There was a Smith listed in the Roanoke city directory, as an aircraft consultant. We knew our Smith flew his own plane and that his firm did a lot of business in the Roanoke area.

"The Smith in Virginia didn't like politics, hated politics, wouldn't talk politics. Understandable, since political people of one state know people in neighboring states. Anyway, we handed photos of our Smith to this Virginia-Smith's neighbors. They said, 'Aw, that's ol' Mary Smith's husband.' We found a babysitter who, while at their house, had looked at a college yearbook. Mary's picture was in there, the sitter said, from a town that began with 'Green. . . .' She could not recall the entire name.

"Our Smith was running for office, which meant the State Elections Board had a filing form with his signature on it. We got hold of the lease on his Roanoke house from the real estate agency that owned it. We took both documents to an expert who said he felt the signatures were by the same person; they sure looked that way to us.

"We checked the birth certificates of the two kids in the family. W. Thomas Smith was listed as the father.

"So far, this was all done with records and other checking. We hadn't touched Smith yet.

"We checked his home airport and found out about flight plans he had filed. We checked Roanoke flight records to see when he was there. And it so happened that the plane had been damaged in a Roanoke windstorm. The airport had had to call Mr. Smith who's the owner. The phone number they called was the one listed for the Roanoke house.

"We had it pretty well tied together at this point; we knew we had the right guy. But we wanted to have the evidence so tight that there wouldn't be any wiggle room. So we kept going, all still in the records, where it was readily available to anyone who wanted to check it.

"We decided we didn't know enough about the Roanoke wife. We phoned Greenville, South Carolina; Greensboro,

North Carolina. We ran the Green . . . into the ground, and we found that this Mary was a former beauty queen at a certain college. At one time she had worked in the state capital for an association that included Smith's firm among its members. She was a secretary there while he was there serving in the General Assembly. He dealt, of course, with this association.

"Now we've got the story and we're safe. But just to make sure, we see if we can run down another Tom Smith who looks alike and has all other characteristics matching. This, of course, is a blind alley. No one matches. We're trying to be real careful about the investigation; we've turned over a lot of rocks and yet we were trying to keep the lid on, because we wanted the exclusive.

"Our plan was to hit them at the same pre-arranged hour with what we knew, so they couldn't get together on their stories by phone. I was to go to Mary's house in Roanoke and people from our office were to go to his home to see Smith.

"We knew Smith had not married Mary. He was not a big-amist. So she knew all about the set-up and would not be surprised at *what* we were telling her, only *that* we were telling her. We knocked on the door, identified ourselves and said we wanted to talk to her. We asked her questions such as where we could find Tom. She was real calm, and just said, 'Well, he goes out of town and I don't always know where to reach him or when he'll be back.' This is known as softening her up; we ask questions that indicate to her we know something but we don't tell her right off what it is we know.

"I showed her a picture of Smith. She, knowing Smith had never allowed his picture to be taken in Virginia, knew we must be showing her a picture from our state. She said, 'You know, it's amazing how much he looks like my husband.'

"It was when I asked her if that was her car in the drive-way and she said yes, that I got to her. I asked her if she knew it was registered to such-and-such firm in our state. She looked as if I had hit her in the pit of the stomach and said she would not answer any more questions. But we knew she knew.

"Meanwhile, in our state, our counterparts had found that Smith was at a precinct meeting in a house on a dead-end street.

So the two reporters just pulled their car crossways so he could not get out of there. When he left the house, they asked him over for a chat. Based on what we had dictated from Roanoke, they began asking questions. And he just said, 'Look, fellas, let's quit playing games. You've got me.' It was just that straightforward and simple.

"We wrote about our encounter with Mary, and the other boys wrote about finding Smith. I'll never forget the lead they put on that piece: 'We found Tom Smith on a dead-end street.' "

6

The Litmus Test:

Deciding When a Story is Justified

---

*"Striking out used to bother the hell
out of me . . . and I finally realized
this was the nature of the work."*

One more phone call. Sometimes that's all it takes to collapse a story a reporter has been working on for weeks. It falls apart like wet tissue.

One more look at what the story is all about. Sometimes that's all it takes to make a reporter realize this is an article that need not even be written.

These are the two ways a story must be justified: on the basis of the evidence and on the basis of the subject.

There's no question that it is a disappointing experience for an investigative reporter to have to jettison a story; it might even be a devastating experience, depending on how long he spent collecting his material or on how much the boss was expecting from the allocation of the reporter's time.

But getting caught in an error, with a flimsy story or with a justified accusation of scandalmongering is far more devastating. Investigative reporting is a specialty which when properly done brings luster to the entire organization. If there is a blunder, however, all departments bear the embarrassment of error. In short, a newspaper's or broadcasting station's standing is not achieved by its recipes or its weather reports but is made by the depth of its reporting.

On The Basis of The Subject

In some instances, a reporter may know his evidence for a story is solid; he may know his audience would avidly follow every detail; yet he may still choose to forgo the article. He does so because his story involves a person's private life rather than his official conduct. Just what is fair game and where do reporters veer into sensationalism? Sometimes the distinction is a fine one.

One writer has described the issue as that of the public's right to know versus its need to know. Few people would question that an officeholder who is taking bribes or extorting payoffs should be exposed. If the same politician instead has a reputation for constant adultery, his constituents may still have the right to know, but do they really benefit from that knowledge? Is it relevant to their appraisal of him as a public official? Should reporters be expected to produce and print that information?

Something Reportable

Media observers agree that there is an unwritten law among reporters that drinking, sex and touchy health items (such as senility) are rarely reported. Journalists often are aware when these problems exist, yet until something "reportable" occurs, these situations do not surface. The something "reportable" is defined by one top investigative reporter as something that can be related to poor performance in office, something on the record (i.e., an arrest for drunk driving) or a wide gap between what the official piously mouths as proper conduct and what he himself actually does.

The former editor of a leading newspaper says he always asked himself why he should print anything of a private nature. "If I happen to find out that my next door neighbor is engaged in marital hankypanky, it may be perfectly true, but what's the point in running it? I think there has to be some point, some reason. The reasons, of course, can be many, but I think it's perfectly proper to ask 'Why?' "

Using these criteria, it's easy to see why former Congressman Wilbur Mills' adventures with the "Argentine Firecracker" remained unknown until the police entered the case. Washington reporters admitted they knew of Mills' drinking problem and even of his clandestine relationship with Fanne Foxe, yet until the duo hit the Tidal Basin and the police blotter, their escapades went unreported. Numerous other instances also can be cited. Reporters interviewed on a television program dealing with the "private lives of public people" listed one story after another they kept undercover. President Jack Kennedy's reputation as a womanizer was a prime example. Even in the situations where reporters said they had not known, some still claimed they would not have produced stories in any event. President Franklin Roosevelt's relationship with Lucy Mercer was such an instance.

In the case of former Rep. Wayne Hays of Ohio, *The Washington Post* was able to run the story not because of Elizabeth Ray's charges of sexual involvement per se but because she was convincing in her charges that she had no secretarial skills and was put on the public payroll merely as a mistress. This was a particularly clear instance where private life and public interest had merged.

In the 1976 Senate campaign in Michigan, however, another celebrated case arose which illustrated how easy it is for reporting on a man's private life to degenerate into mudslinging. Donald H. Riegle, Jr., a Democratic congressman who later won the Senate seat, was accused by *The Detroit News* of an affair seven years earlier with an unpaid worker in his congressional office. The printing of tape-recorded conversations between Riegle and the woman, identified at first only as Dorothy, added an especially lurid touch. The *News* excused its stories on the basis that "people have a right to know what kind of man is asking for their votes." There was no other relevance to the stories about the affair.

Difficulties with alcohol are another area where the media should tread carefully.

"Unless the alcoholism is a blatant thing," says a reporter, "it's one of those gray areas. I personally am not qualified to say who is an alcoholic or not."

In a recent congressional campaign, for example, a candidate charged that the incumbent had been seen drunk in Washington and had stumbled on the floor of the House. These charges were printed by a major newspaper in his congressional district. The paper contacted the incumbent's colleagues in the House to get their comments on the congressman's drinking habits. None gave a flat statement about his drinking, and their answers could be variously interpreted. The newspaper did not substantiate the charges but merely tossed them out for its readers' notice. Several days later, the same paper carried a story that the son of the candidate making the charges had been accused of drunken driving the previous summer and had pleaded guilty to careless and reckless driving. Exactly what this belated report had to do with his father's qualifications was unclear. The paper was permitting itself to print articles which were unjustified as news or as relevant material.

One newsman discussed the dangers of accusing someone of being a drunk even when the fact is common knowledge. "Let's suppose I write the story, and I am the only one who does write that 'So-and-So showed up on the House floor drunk yesterday.' Drunk is a judgment. It isn't a fact since he hasn't been tried and convicted in court. It's my estimation. I can say he lurched or fell down or stuttered or stammered, but if I say he turned up drunk, half the guys on the floor who yesterday were telling me, 'Isn't it awful the way he's acting; I'm so embarrassed I don't know what to do,' are going to take the floor and defend him to the limits when my article shows up. I will be denounced for having said such heinous things about their esteemed colleague, the gentleman from such-and-such county. So here I am, making an accusation I have no way to prove."

Adds a newswoman speaking of another such case, "All he (the official) would do is claim he'd suddenly been taken dizzy and needed those cold compresses and coffee."

Saying what a person did, rather than characterizing the situation, seems to be the favored way of dealing with the matter.

"I had an editor who used to tell us to say what the man did and let the readers draw their own conclusions," says one reporter. "I try not to deal in people's private lives any more than absolutely necessary."

Another reason reporters claim they are slow to report such "hot skinny," as one editor terms it, is because their superiors require a higher degree of proof in such cases or because they have had their bosses say no to attempts to release such information.

"We had one official who earned the nickname 'Grog' because he drank so much," recalls a newsman. "I remember one time when he had to crown a beauty queen. All those girls walking around in bathing suits, and he was getting ribald. The state police got him out of there fast. If he had stayed and fallen off the platform, that would have been reported." Whether the reason for his fall would have been included, however, is conjecture.

Even in cases where the problem clearly is pegged to malfeasance in office or to a specific incident, many reporters still decline to make the situation public.

"We've had some notorious drunks in our legislature, and it was very easy to prove," says an editor. "One man used to be dried out periodically in a hospital near the Capitol. There would have been no problem proving it. But it wasn't written about because despite his drinking, he was still probably one of the best legislators we had. I would have taken him drunk over the rest of them sober. And just the fact that someone else is a drunk and not a very good legislator doesn't justify a story to me."

Another reporter remembers a legislator who was a steady drinker, often appearing on the floor inebriated. "But I never wrote the story because he was just keeping the seat warm anyway. The constituents were getting cheated when he was sober as well as when he was drunk, so they weren't losing anything."

Furthermore, when something quite "reportable" happens, the same newsmen who claim they are waiting for just such an event quite often renege. In one state, for instance, even when a known drinker, arguing in a committee hearing against liberalizing liquor laws, was berated for his "do as I say, not as I do" attitude, not a single correspondent released the story. Similarly, a Washington editor admits that a drunken congressman on the floor is news, but adds that he hasn't printed such incidents.

There are similar situations, however, where most editors agree that the personal conduct is so relevant it cannot be ignored.

The cases of Sen. Edward Kennedy and Sen. Thomas Eagleton are well-known ones which reveal most editors' convictions that where the Presidency or Vice Presidency is involved, moral or health issues are vital stories.

"It's one thing to be a senator and chase women, but it's something else to do this as President," says one reporter about Ted Kennedy's Chappaquidick auto accident in which a woman passenger drowned. "If he is a potential presidential candidate, I think anything about a man, his political ideas, anything relating to his character, his health, his capacity to serve in public office, is something that people are entitled to know. Now if it is just some hankypanky with a female, I would not necessarily report it. It's only when the thing becomes pertinent. Chappaquidick was so pertinent because to some extent like Watergate, it was not the original event itself, but the apparent attempted coverup which made it so important. Chappaquidick would have been a one-day sensation without that coverup."

Sen. Thomas Eagleton was the initial nominee for Vice President on the Democratic ticket in 1972 but was bumped from that spot when his history of treatment for mental illness was publicized. "I think the press handled that story well," says one reporter. "They went after it. It was a personal misfortune, his need for mental treatment, but under the circumstances, you couldn't just ignore it, it was a factor. There was a reason for doing it: he might be President one day."

Sen. Eagleton was also the subject of stories by investigative reporter Jack Anderson who accused him of having been charged with drunken driving even though no records of the charges existed. "If it had been true," says another newsman, "that a man running for Vice President had a sufficient drinking problem so that he had in fact been arrested four or five times for drunken driving, then I would say that is a pertinent fact that the American people ought to know. The trouble with Anderson is that he went off half-cocked, and for that he deserves all the criticism he got." Anderson went ahead with the Eagleton story without documentation, because he had been promised photostats of records which had allegedly been destroyed. He later retracted the story because he could not obtain proof of the accusations. "But if the story had been fairly investigated and was true, then I think it would have been pertinent. I think that in judging who I am going to vote for, the fact that a person is an alcoholic is a factor I am entitled to know, even though I might decide, like Abraham Lincoln allegedly did about General Grant, to find out what brand of whiskey he drinks and give it to all the generals."

Families of Officials

An even touchier point is whether it's fair or newsworthy, for example, to write a big story about a young man hooked on drugs just because his father is a candidate for public office. Does his son's lifestyle affect his father? Will it influence the way the father handles his job, particularly in regard to drug laws or programs? If an official's wife has cancer and prefers to keep it a secret, should the news media refuse to honor her wish? Can a reporter decide whether the pressures of a wife's illness are affecting the man's performance? Is it the public's business if a congressman has a brother who's run out on his creditors? Should the public know if a Vice President's son is a homosexual?

Although public officials have willingly placed themselves in the limelight and may be expected to undergo scrutiny of any sort, their families may be unwilling victims.

The guideline in deciding whether to expose family problems of a public figure, suggests one reporter, is "Can they influence events?" The wife of a President, for example, could both directly and indirectly create problems if she were an alcoholic. She would be in many delicate diplomatic situations where her actions might both embarrass and compromise the United States. By this criterion, the documented drinking excesses of any candidate's wife would be legitimate copy. Joan Kennedy has been written about numerous times for her visits to emotional treatment centers. In her case, the Kennedy name is sufficient to draw attention whether she has any significant influence on her husband's position as senator.

"There's Always Something"

"If an alderman is sleeping with someone on the side, I don't want to know that stuff. It makes me nervous, this stuff about how reporters are going to have to poke into the private lives of public figures," says a reporter. "If we do that, then Nixon would have been justified to go poking into our private lives."

Whether the novice agrees with that reporter or with the newswoman who feels that whatever an official does eventually shows up in his public performance ("Even if it's just the effect of the late hours"), he must consider the issue, for it is one he will eventually confront.

Willie Stark, a character in *All the King's Men* by Robert Penn Warren, tells his aide that it's always possible to dig up embarrassing or scandalous material on people: "Man is conceived in sin and born in corruption and he passeth from the stink of the didie to the stench of the shroud. There is always something."

ON THE BASIS OF THE EVIDENCE

No excesses of fancy can be permitted in the investigative piece; nothing may be charged without documentation. The story has got to be there.

But how does a journalist know when the story is indeed justified on the basis of the evidence?

There are several factors which the beginning reporter must consider in trying to decide if he is ready to go with his story: (1) Is it a story at all? (2) Does the evidence reveal that the original tip was faulty? (3) Is there a story there, but one which can't be sufficiently proved?

Is It a Story?

Sometimes it's difficult to determine if a possible piece is, even with all necessary information, a story at all. Or is it something to which a reader would respond, "So what?" All articles, particularly investigative ones, must have a point. If there's no point or angle, you've got no story, even though you have data. And that's an important consideration. An almanac, dictionary and atlas have data. But their contents are not stories; there's no point. You must have information which can be assembled with a "peg" before you are ready to roll.

Here's an example of an idea which might seem to be a story but really is not. A reporter had permission to check through a religious organization's files and found a letter written by a civic leader in which the man made anti-Semitic statements. The man was now running for public office. Question: What should the reporter do with what he'd found?

In this case he did nothing. "What would have been my peg? The only thing I could have written would have been 'So-and-So denied today that he is anti-Semitic, despite a letter in his own handwriting which this paper turned up.' I hate those stories starting off with a denial, and that's the only way this story could have been written, and that's just not a peg. All you've got is my assertion that he is anti-Semitic because I've stumbled on it, and he would say, 'No, because my letter was written in the heat of passion; I was upset when I wrote it; and show me some concrete example of where I've been anti-Semitic.' It's the kind of story the reader would have read and said, 'Damn, that paper is trying something.' It would have created more sympathy for the subject of the piece. A lot of this is feel, part of experience; a news peg is something that *is,* rather than an opinion. I just didn't have enough—no overt action on his part to demonstrate that he was anti-Semitic. If I had found a Ku Klux Klan record with his name on the membership rolls, a document, proof that he had *acted* in a certain way, then I would have gone with it. And let him deny it if he wanted to. You just have to weigh each individual case.''

A person's position sometimes provides a news peg. Stories have to be evaluated not only on the basis of what is being said, but also on who is doing the talking. While a low-ranking company or government official may know as much as the top people, the story is much more forceful if told by a top figure.

One reporter came across a story about the way a utility was being run and about its contributions to political campaign chests and slush funds. The source was a very high-ranking officer who had been fired from the utility. But even here the circumstances gave the reporter pause.

''It raised some ethical questions in my mind. Here was a guy obviously with an axe to grind, who said things that were very damaging to people and he brought us very little actual documentation to back it up. And we gave him two-and-a-half pages in our paper to say just about anything he wanted to. We wouldn't do that for a junior executive at this utility without giving it a hell of a lot more consideration.

''But I tell you why we did it. Because a guy of this rank who tells you things comes along only once in a while. Here's a guy who had been in all those meetings you (had only) suspected were being held. Here's a guy who was in a place and a position to know what was going on. He had good reason to know what was going on—it was part of his job as general manager and vice president, to massage the politicians and make sure the right guy got elected governor.

''So he wasn't the average person and we took this position: we're going to check out everything possible and where we can verify we're going to say so and what we can't verify we will say so too. Very high in the story we ran there is a paragraph that says exactly that—that some of this stuff may not be right and we point out what the guy's problems are—that he got fired, his marriage was breaking up, he had not located another job and so on. But that was the only way the story could ever be broken. And chances are there won't be another guy along like him for a while.''

Shun Salvage Operations

There's an interesting force at work in lengthy investigations: the strong tendency to make something from the research even when the original tip or thesis simply wasn't accurate. Somehow it seems that after all the weeks and months of talking to person after person, there must be something that can be salvaged to make a story and justify the effort.

Some reporters (and their editors or news directors) try to force a story, refusing to cut their losses. "I've seen stories that passed for investigative reporting but in my judgment there wasn't a story there," says a reporter. "I guess it was a justification for a man's work. I don't say these were fabrications, just nonstories."

This type of production might be called the "no-Podunkville-people-were-involved-in-the-Watergate-scandal" school of reporting. And running such nonstories (who ever suspected anyone from little ol' Podunkville to be involved? And sure enough, no one was!) is counterproductive. Readers or listeners vaguely feel the reporting is not solid, not quite trustworthy. The public senses that the particular news outlet is "making" news.

One former investigative reporter, now an editor of a major state paper, thinks objectivity and maturity are called for in the decision of whether a story can be finished. "It's hard, after you spend five or six weeks investigating . . . . It's tempting to try to recover something out of the story even though you don't have the real story. I think it requires a certain amount of maturity at some level, on either the reporter's or the editor's part, to simply say, 'Let's cut our losses on this one; we've invested some time, but the story is not there,' and then pull back. There's also the factor that the longer you pursue the story the greater the chances of its becoming almost like an obsession. You have to be able to look at yourself objectively and say, 'Wait a minute, am I willing to accept the facts as they are?' "

Failure to produce a story is difficult for most investigative reporters to accept. But such a possibility must be recognized or inaccurate, flimsy articles will result.

Says one reporter of his experiences in learning the ropes:

"I can't tell you how many times I struck out . . . and it used to bother the hell out of me. I'd feel guilty. And finally I realized this was the nature of the work. You gotta strike out; you just have to. Sometimes it seems you have excellent leads, but things are misinterpreted; there was no story there to begin with."

"There were times when I had a damned good story," adds another journalist. "And I was ready to sit down and write it and it would sing. But then I'd make one more telephone call because I felt I had to touch one more base. I'd ask one more question. Pow! There went the story. And you want to kick yourself. But then, you know, well, that's the way it has to be. Because that's part of being a fair, honest reporter. I don't pretend to be unbiased and unprejudiced, but I try to be fair and honest. And when you lose the story by asking one more question, you chalk it off."

Can I Prove It?

The reporter, no matter how strongly he feels his conclusions to be true, must objectively decide if the evidence backs him up. When an investigative piece is run, it simply cannot bear errors. The victim of an exposé will be only too quick to jump on one faulty conclusion and use it to discredit the validity of the entire charge. Even minor mistakes can be parlayed into cries of sloppy reporting.

One way to head off errors is to constantly recheck material: one record against another; one person's recollection against another's; records and people against each other.

"You keep asking, 'Is there anything to this or is it a lot of bull?' " a veteran says. Where there are doubts and the subject is potentially explosive, "then you have to have absolute verification or as close as you can get to absolute."

"And if it is a very serious story, you not only check it as much as you can, but you get your firm's lawyers to look at it too, particularly if you are a big paper and have a great deal to lose in case of a libel suit," notes a cautious editor.

Among the most difficult stories to pin down are kickbacks or bribes. Generally only two people are involved—the giver and the taker—and neither is likely to blab. The payoff is usually in cash and thus not traceable. There are no records. You may be able to show that the person who had something to gain got the same benefit as he might have gotten via a bribe, but you may not be able to show that a bribe was actually made.

Stories about evil motives are also difficult to document. You may feel certain a congressman helped defeat a crucial bill because he hated its sponsor, yet without hard evidence such a speculation is difficult to substantiate.

Thus you must constantly ask yourself if the story can be obtained. "There's a 'probability system' which works in your head and says, 'Okay, it's 70-30 that you can make this story. Are there records; how many people will be in on this?' Or, it may be there, but I could spend months on it, and the probability of making it is only 20-80. Instead, I see one that's 70-30 in my favor that's got a quick payoff so I go ahead and do that one," says one investigative reporter.

Here are a few checkpoints to consider in weighing your evidence: (1) Hypothetically, could I go into court and use my facts to convince a jury "beyond a reasonable doubt"? Maybe I don't have all the holes filled, but can I admit they exist without substantially weakening my main points? (2) Am I able to write this story in a straightforward manner? Or am I relying on rhetoric to convince the reader? If so, the facts themselves are too flimsy. (3) Would I be embarrassed if I had to reveal the names and extent of my sources? Although I am willing where necessary to protect sources, am I confident that the sources are truly reliable where I credit them with being so? Have I asked people on all sides of the issue for comment? Do I say "many" when I mean two or three? Do I use the word "survey" when actually I checked with a couple of contacts? (4) Do I have to scour my notes for a quote which I can contort into meaning what I want it to?

If the answers to these questions aren't satisfactory, then re-examine the situation before writing the story.

One final way of deciding if the proper evidence has been assembled is by "feel." Experienced reporters know when they're ready to move. Although this checkpoint is unavailable to the novice, he can call on editors and colleagues for guidance and appraisal. In the beginning, he can see how they evaluate their own material, and gradually he will develop the ability to sense when to begin to write.

"It's hard to pinpoint it," says a reporter, "but on every story you reach the moment when you know whether the story is there or not. It gets to be a feeling. There have been cases where I've rushed into print too fast and gotten embarrassed—not by being totally wrong but by missing some things or being a little off on some details. Then people hit you on those details."

CASE HISTORIES OF TWO ABANDONED STORIES

Case A

In this first story, note: (1) how the reporter worked to find out as much as he could in the records; (2) how the hard evidence still eluded him; (3) how the principals were able to deny the questions; and (4) how he resigned himself to abandoning the idea.

"I was working on a story that involved kickback payments on the purchase of parking meters for a small town. I started working on it because I was talking over a beer one night with a fellow who was a traffic engineer in another town. He said that anytime parking meters were sold to a town, kickbacks were always offered. The kickback might be rejected, but he said it was just the way business was done to offer it. Just part of the trade.

"I asked him, 'How can I tell if this is being done in my town?' and he said, 'If you see too many parking meters on side streets, you are probably getting a good indication.' He went on to explain that initially a town is talked into getting meters for its productive central city area. When those produce a lot of revenue, the meter firm reappears and says, 'Since those are making so much, get more for other spots.' The only thing is, that the farther you get from the high-demand parking area, the less revenue will be produced. But the town council feels like the additional meters are being paid for by the profits of the first ones and since it does not require money diverted from other funds, they agree. The parking meter firm has then sold lots more meters than necessary, and they are also locked into all the replacement parts business.

"In this case, we tried going to the records, to get figures on the revenue produced by the meters. Revenue is not usually listed per meter, but you can detect patterns. For instance, if in 1970 100 meters made $50 each, but in 1975 300 meters produced only $25 each, obviously the net amount per meter decreased as the number increased. This is because the outlying meters can't produce like the ones downtown. So the question is: why did the council invest in them?

"Town council records showed that the first meters were bought under what looked like very competitive selection. Lots of council discussion, several bidders. But once the type was chosen, the council is actually locked in to the producing firm for replacement parts and so on. There was also some competition later for replacements and additions to the first meters. Invariably the initial company will get the successive business, even when they submit the high bid, because city officials can take the higher bid if there are extenuating circumstances as to why they chose it. So they justify it by saying, 'Well, compatibility of parts, etc., demands that we take this firm again.' And ultimately you see that in bidding situations like these the price of meters can rise on successive purchases, because they know the city is committed to them. Similar things can happen with two-way radio equipment for law enforcement agencies or other hardware.

"I scoured around to find out about the salesman for the parking meter company. I asked other towns about their experiences with the fellow. No one would say for public consumption, but they did admit he wasn't above offering a cut to the decision-maker. And when the parking meter salesman was in town he always was very friendly with the city manager, having drinks and dinner together. But that's not enough to make a story on.

"In this particular town, the city manager was the purchasing agent and his recommendations carried great weight with the council. We then looked into the records to check on any big personal purchases made by the city manager recently. We, of course, couldn't get his bank records, but we checked for liens recorded on major credit purchases of furniture or a car and whether he had been involved in any land acquisitions or very favorable sales. We did find that he had bought a beach house after the second or third installation of these meters. But still that's not a solid enough connection. There was simply nothing on the records showing anything illegal or improper, but we were still suspicious of the purchase of those unnecessary meters.

"We decided we just had to confront the manager and the meter company, separately, in an attempt to put it to them straight and try to get a lead from the conversation to spring it out of them.

"We asked the city manager straight, 'You've got all these meters, costing more than they take in, why did you recommend buying them?' The manager was cool. 'The revenue was not crucial,' he said. 'We were trying to get traffic control, to keep it flowing.' We then asked him about his relationship with the salesman, and he acknowledged the dinners, saying that he worked better then and that he did not let the other fellow pick up the check any more than he did.

"So we tried the meter company. They were reluctant to talk at first. We tried to find improper influence—trips, vacations, conventions to Las Vegas for the manager. They denied spending a nickel that way.

"We also talked to the other parking meter firms that had submitted bids. They said it was crucial to be the firm chosen to put in the first meters as the future business was virtually assured. No, they did not know what this other salesman offered, but they knew he was a hustler. We got nothing concrete from them. Remember, my original source had said they all did business this way, so it would have been no real gain for them to blow the whistle on others, because everyone might be revealed. Unless a fellow was really disgruntled about someone else getting the contract, no one would talk.

"We could assume the city manager was either not too bright, or got conned by a fast talker, or he did get bribed. And the scheme, if that's what it was, would eventually end anyway, because you run out of streets that you can legitimately defend meters for—it's hard to run them along a rural two-lane road.

"So, we had suspicions; we thought strongly something was wrong. We tried to spring it, but everyone held. So you fold your notebook and go home.

"This story is a good example of how if two people are doing something immoral or illegal, but doing it in cash, it's virtually impossible to prove unless one of them gets mad and turns informer.

"This account of my failure is not meant to discourage other people from trying. You run a number of cases where the assumption probably wasn't true to begin with; other cases are 50-50; in others you are missing one key piece even after much legwork. If you hit one in five that's a pretty high percentage."

Case B

And, almost to prove that one reporter can encounter multiple failures, the reporter quoted above described another experience where he had to jettison a story after he couldn't get the evidence needed. In this instance, he ran into a stone wall that could not be gotten over or around.

"When the path for a new highway is decided, it's generally kept secret until time comes to announce it. In this case, right after designation of a highway was made public, rumors were running that a highway official had been trading in the land along the proposed route.

"Again we went to the records, trying to find any record of land transfers in his name, or those of his family members or close business associates. None showed; we dropped it. But the rumors persisted, so we picked it up again.

"We decided to approach it from the other end. Instead of tracing the man, we would research the land that changed hands along the path recently and match this up for names. Now, the really valuable land along a limited access road, which this was, is the interchange spots for gas stations, motels, shopping centers and such. The land next to the roadway but without access is not valuable.

"Two pieces of land in large tracts in the interchange spots had changed ownership in the previous 12 months. We found that the land was held in the name of a closed corporation, a newly formed one. We tried to find out who owned it and ran it, by going to the secretary of state's office in the state capital. We found the papers, but they listed the names of a lawyer and his two secretaries. This is perfectly legal. He is acting as a representative for his client in signing the incorporation papers. This is where a lot of investigative reporting bogs down; if the lawyer and his office staff stand pat you can't get below that level. Now closed corporations may file additional papers specifying their agents or such, but they don't have to. The incorporation papers themselves may or may not help you. The lawyer can pay bills in the corporation's name and conduct business for it, and you never learn who is behind it.

"The records showed no resale of this land bought by the corporation, and unless the true owner was willing to deal personally with the purchaser, the lawyer could sell that on behalf of the corporation, too. So you might pick up something in a resale, but don't bet on it.

"We finally put it to the lawyer. But he pleaded lawyer-client confidentiality, and of course his office staff wouldn't talk.

"I did know the lawyer had previously handled the highway official's legal affairs and that they were political buddies. But that still isn't proof of anything. We were dead.

"We went to the highway official. Asked him if he had made any purchases along the right-of-way. He denied it outright. He also denied being in the corporation.

"Whether he lied or not, we'll never know. But you never know what you will come up with until you put your nickel in the slot and see what you get out."

This same reporter points out that not in all cases does the investigative reporter have to have rock-hard evidence of wrongdoing to run a story about the circumstances.

"Where events present such strong presumption that it's impossible for a public official to operate at arm's length with the firms or people he deals with in his post, you can just report it because he should be put in the position of proving or explaining how it is he can operate objectively after these other things have occurred. Now maybe this stuff he's done is not truly illegal; it's just immoral or unethical or plain bad judgment. But if he decides who gets water permits or such and he buys a piece of coastal land for himself from a real estate developer who needs those permits, how can the developer sell him the land without a price break? And even if it is sold to the guy at a legitimate price, it looks terrible and arouses questions in the mind of the town's other residents. So the assumption of guilt shifts from the reporter having to prove something onto the official involved when that official has benefited in some way from his public acts. If you go this route, however, you must have your circumstances down pat; he cannot be able to offer an alibi that sounds reasonable enough to cover for him."

7

Trial Balloons and Other Four-Letter Words:

Recognizing the News Manipulator

*"The reporters largely deserve what they get . . .
if they are stupid enough to be
manipulated time after time, they deserve it."*

You have the news manipulators always with you.

And covering them is a different proposition from doing an investigative piece on someone or something you'll probably never encounter again. News manipulators usually are found in permanent, or at least semi-permanent, positions in politics or business. They are sources you'll be forced to return to again and again.

News manipulators come from different fields, but all have the same goal: to have publicized *what* they want publicized *when* they want it publicized. The most obvious manipulators are the politician and the government official. Lobbyists also are in the group, as are public relations people and campaign press secretaries. Other manipulators are not so easily discernible. Company presidents, university chancellors and attorneys acting for their clients all dabble in the art of press manipulation at one time or other. Occasionally a manipulator will conduct himself with such dignity that he'll be able to lead editors and reporters to accept and report his perception of a story. He can feed tips that are swallowed whole, whereas the same guidance offered by others less subtle will be received skeptically.

None of these people is automatically wicked in pursuing his goal, but he is seeking the most advantageous position for the person, company or institution that pays his salary. The reporter will find that when expedience demands it, some of these people will lie and most will evade or hedge.

Motives for the duplicity vary, ranging all the way from protecting someone against a minor embarrassment, to trying to sway public opinion, to denying criminal wrongdoing to fend off an indictment.

Obviously no good reporter will knowingly permit himself to be manipulated. But the problem is rarely clear-cut. For example, when reporter and manipulator deal with each other on a continuing basis chumminess can develop. When it does, it's usually the public that loses. Rarely will being overfriendly harm the manipulator. Too close a personal relationship permits the manipulator to tell the reporter inside stories, plans and opinions, secure in the knowledge that the reporter "understands" and will never write a word. Sometimes the reporter and manipulator assure each other that "It's better for the public not to know." Such a friendship also may lead the reporter to tell what he's learned elsewhere to this friend and become an unwitting informer.

Even without overt coziness, beat reporters face other types of manipulation. They become prisoners of the system. If the journalist pursues something unfavorable, officials may become angry and dry up sources or give wrong leads.

One reporter, for example, recounted a colleague's battle with the governor's office.

"There was a tip that the governor had maliciously quashed a promotion for a highway patrolman. That's what this reporter was told, and he believed it. He never checked it out on his own. An enemy of the governor was trying to stick it to the governor and told the reporter this story, but not for direct quotation. When the reporter tried to contact the governor's office for comments on the situation, they wouldn't even talk to him.

"So he went ahead and wrote the story. And the next day the governor's office put out a release saying the printed version was all wrong—and they laid out the right story. It turned out that the governor had a legitimate reason for denying promotion—under law there were no slots left to promote the guy to, even though he was deserving. The list was closed to all patrolmen. The reporter had been set up. He was double-set up—first by the people who wanted to put their version of the story in the paper and who didn't tell him the whole story, and then by the governor's office getting back at a reporter they didn't like. They could have told him the right stuff when he asked, but they figured he had stuck them so many times they would let him fry. And he fried."

Occasionally after an annoying story is run, an executive will issue a fiat that no employee is to speak to the press, on pain of firing. This kind of retaliation rarely lasts long (for one thing, people just won't shut up), but it's always a reminder that reporters are dependent on the people they are covering for information.

If an official is angry at a particular reporter, he can refuse or delay interviews, withhold information or set up favorable things for the reporter's competition. Presidents, for example, can attempt to make the press dance to their tune by denying White House credentials or travel credentials or by granting exclusive interviews to a competitor. The last is the unkindest cut of all.

In this chapter we will discuss some now-established additions to the information scene—the news conference, news release and news secretary, as well as the devious tactics which sometimes result in a careless reporter finding himself being used for someone else's ends. Most examples cited will deal with politicians and/or government officials, because these two have virtually constant contact with the media and are experts in leading reporters to water and making them drink. The same principles and criticisms, however, apply to lobbyists, company presidents, university chancellors, et. al., when they engage in similar activities.

ORGANIZED MANIPULATION

Propaganda. The term dates from the 17th Century and the establishment of the College of Propaganda by the Catholic church to propagate the faith. The news manipulators are intent on publishing their propaganda in some form. Several devices designed to do so have come into common use.

News Conferences

These are large gatherings, assembled by the interviewee in a place usually of his choosing, at a time usually of his choosing, to release information and/or possibly to entertain questions. News conferences do have some merit: if the person involved is a high government official or national politician, the conference at least provides a chance to ask questions face to face, an opportunity unavailable to the average journalist. But news conferences inherently contain numerous disadvantages.

One drawback of such gatherings is that a reporter gets to pose only one question without follow-up. He cannot force the subject to clarify vague or evasive answers.

"News conferences are basically a fabrication," says one reporter. "The guy gets a group of reporters and he gives an answer full of bull but he doesn't come back to you and you can't get back to him."

This same reporter is not enthusiastic about any off-the-record answers, but especially scoffs at the idea of their use in a news conference. "Anytime there are lots of people involved, it's a joke, because how do you know who to trust and who not to trust? In a public news conference, I just don't accept an off-the-record thing. I will tell the guy, 'Just don't say it, if you're going to go off the record at all.' "

One newspaper editor feels a news conference's value depends on how it's set up, noting that presidential ones have become "staged spectaculars. Television has had a lot to do with running news conferences because the guy is acting for TV, and that has made it all a lot less productive than it used to be.

"At the same time, if you have a news conference run by

someone who knows how to use a news conference and if there's some coherence in the thing instead of just letting it wander all over hell, it serves a useful purpose. With some people, the only way you can get at them is through a news conference. How do you get at the governor these days unless you go to a news conference. If you've got a question to ask, you get an opportunity to raise it and you may catch him unawares. The subject is mainly interested in using a news conference to his own advantage, naturally, but you don't have to let it stop there. You've got your own little fish to fry when you get in there.''

In an effort to get even tighter control over the conference, some people call ''one-topic'' news conferences. The governor, for example, wants to announce that a major firm has just moved into the state; he does not want to take questions on the reported rift between himself and his closest political mentor or on whether Commissioner XYZ is going to be dismissed. If the journalists agree to this arrangement (and showing up indicates agreeement), the subject of the ''news conference'' has the best of all possible worlds: he gets reported just what he wants, on his terms. These shenanigans should really not be termed a ''news'' conference at all; they are really publicity announcements. Sometimes a few reporters will try to ask questions about other items anyway. They are quickly reprimanded that this is, after all, a one-topic session.

Why do reporters attend governmental press conferences if they are less than optimum ways of getting news? Realistically, no news outlet is going to get beaten on the story anyway because the wire services assign a staff member to cover. But old-fashioned competition rules the day. If A-town has a staff byline report of the governor's news conference, then B-town's editor wants to know from his capital bureau man why *he* didn't file a story instead of relying on the wire. To protect themselves, 20 reporters waste their time on an event that probably will produce nothing newsworthy.

News Releases

News organizations receive reams of releases every year; most wind up in the wastepaper basket. But government, industry and businesses still keep at least one staff member (sometimes a battalion) grinding out the gospel according to that institution. Although releases can be of interest, such as those outlining a new development or expansion, rarely do they offer more than routine news or puffery. Releases, however, are firmly established as an easy way to manipulate the lazy writer or media outlet who sometimes puts the entire release into print or on the air without question.

The smart reporter can sometimes turn the manipulator's own words against him. By collecting releases during a political campaign, for example, a reporter can develop the candidate's "official" position on the issues or quickly find details on how his comments made this morning dispute what he said two months ago.

Clever government officials can also turn the news release back against the reporter. "We were working on a story about our State Bureau of Investigation, and the governor's office knew it. The morning our story broke, they handed out a news release about their own report on the bureau so that it undercut our story and minimized the impact of what we had written," says a newsman. Other media reported both stories in the same wrap-up that day, resulting in a stand-off in the minds of readers or viewers.

News Secretaries

These people operate under a wide variety of titles: public relations officer, information officer, press secretary, liaison officer, etc. All the titles mean the same thing: They are producing the aforementioned news releases, setting up the news conferences and trying to put the best face on what their boss says or does.

News secretaries come in handy for getting around large organizations. Faced with obtaining information from a bureaucracy and with no idea under whose jurisdiction the matter falls, a reporter discovers that the public relations person is the logical starting point. Also, if just a couple of noncontroversial statistics are needed, often the PR person can be an acceptable and speedy source.

The press secretary also sets up interviews, and in those cases where his employers are by nature nervous about reporters he can do a lot to smooth things on each side so that the interview is beneficial to both.

Public relations people also block information, either by handing out their own version of the facts or else serving as a barrier between the reporter and the source he wants to reach. News secretaries are experts, for example, at referring a reporter's question to the source who can handle it best—best that is, from the organization's point of view. The maverick or the bumbler is not brought to the reporter's attention. Thus, while he thinks he is getting the information he needs, it is coming only from a carefully groomed source.

Sometimes both the news secretary and the press are used by the principal, in that false or misleading information is deliberately fed to the news secretary, who hands it out in good faith to the reporter. Such a situation allegedly occurred in President Ford's administration. Gerald terHorst, Ford's first press secretary, cited this type of set-up as the reason he left Ford's staff after one month on the job.

There are some reporters who feel that they can hound the news secretary and that eventually the person will break and reveal lots of information. But a good one will rarely break and the most that nagging can earn is enmity for the persistent journalist. The best news secretaries, in fact, always maintain their composure. One should be aware of this tactic. It is difficult, for example, to insist on an answer to a serious question when the news secretary laughs and indicates that he's surprised at your wasting your time with such a trifle.

News secretaries also toy with the press by helping shape its attitudes. During his presidential campaign, for example, Jimmy Carter's people made it clear from the beginning that he was the underdog. Thus each achievement became a triumph. Predictions of success, on the other hand, were minimized, and Carter's primary losses were not perceived by the media as setbacks because he indicated they were expected. He shaped the coverage of his campaign merely by having his news people perpetuate such stances.

In addition, news secretaries can be disarming by admitting the errors of their organization and throwing themselves on the media's mercy.

Not only do principal sources hedge and evade, their intermediaries do it too. News secretaries slide a great deal by reporters who aren't listening intently.

The reporter may think he's won an answer, but he hasn't really. On one occasion a reporter was trying to dig out information on campaign activities. He first called the candidate, who told him nothing. But the candidate then phoned the news secretary to report the inquiry. When the reporter called the news secretary later in the day, he said, "I guess you heard I have already spoken to (the candidate)." "I've been out most of the day," was the truthful response from the news secretary. That did not answer the question. The reporter never knew the candidate and news secretary had already discussed the matter and that he was not actually getting off-the-cuff responses to his questions.

Hedging and evasion can be carried, like most everything else, too far. During the Nixon administration, relations between the news media and a press secretary reached what must have been an all-time nadir. During a morning briefing in 1971, Ron Ziegler was asked a question and responded in part that "That order has not gone out from here." The questioning reporter got to follow up and said, "Ron, I don't want to be a nitpicker but we've got to watch our terms these days. When you say 'from here' do you mean from the precise spot on the floor where your two feet are, or from this room or do you mean from the Nixon White House?" Ziegler answered he meant the latter. But that was the extent to which suspicion had gone. Ziegler and his staff were, in fact, so skilled at evasion that a *Columbia Journalism Review* article documented his techniques. The article listed these masterly methods of driving newsmen to distraction: the broad and meaningless statement; the I'll-try-to-find-out ploy; the I-stand-on-my-previous-answer answer; the I-wouldn't-join-you-in-the-gutter response; the wild goose chase; and those old favorites—"no comment" and the lie.

One gubernatorial news secretary had a well-worded response to certain questions: "I can't answer that." "Do you mean you can't answer it because you don't know the answer or because you aren't allowed to answer?" one reporter pressed. "I can't answer that," came the reply. It was a shrewd response because if he were uninformed, he never gave away that he was deprived of the information. If he was under orders to say nothing, he never gave away that people "on high" wanted the matter guarded.

His answer has one other thing to recommend it. He wasn't lying. News secretaries would spare themselves a lot of grief if they would learn that a "No comment" or "I can't answer that" is considerably easier for a reporter to deal with than an outright lie. These alternative replies preserve some semblance of credibility.

OTHER TYPES OF MANIPULATION

There are a number of other techniques used by the practiced news manipulator. We will now review several variations on the theme of "giving reporters the slip."

Including the Reporter

This is a slick way to latch onto the reporter's own credibility, and it is used primarily with broadcast reporters who are taping or filming an interview. Speaking quickly, to make it difficult to eliminate the phrase by editing, the interviewee will say, "Well, as you are well aware, Mary, we have been trying for months to get this program approved for the benefit of the city." Or, "John, you know how hard we have been working for this day . . ."

The reporter can hardly blurt out, "No, I am not aware of any such thing" or "I don't know about that at all." Even if the reporter is aware that a certain campaign or drive was announced months back, he has no idea how much effort has been put into it. A reporter may also be brought in on disputes in this manner: "Larry, you've seen how the other side has twisted this thing and how they've played fast and loose with the truth." Comments like this attempt to use the reporter's credibility to advance one side of the issue. The journalist may evade this tactic by completing the filmed or taped interview, and then re-asking the question after explaining to the interviewee that he, as the reporter, must not be referred to in the answer. Back in the studio the film or tape then can be edited to run in the right order. This gimmick is not effective with print reporters because even if a person says it, no reporter with a brain in his head is going to run the entire quote.

Less blatant is another method of including the reporter. As a candidate, Jimmy Carter cleverly sought reporters' advice on various matters. A reporter who's been led to believe he has had input about a vice-presidential contender, for example, will no doubt be friendlier to that choice.

Trial Balloons

This is one of the spots where reporters traditionally get used. Something is passed to a reporter as legitimate information when in actuality the source is trying to test the public's response to the idea. This is used frequently by would-be political candidates who want to run for office but who have not been besieged with supporters. (Has a candidate ever admitted lacking "friends who have urged me to run for this office . . . ?") The office seeker tells a reporter that he is considering a bid for the job. But, he admonishes, the item is to be run without attribution. The public does not know John Doe says John Doe may run for mayor. If Doe gets good response to the idea, he pays his filing fee. If people tell him to forget it, he calls the reporter and denies the possibility. Then the denial runs, and it becomes an error in the grapevine. A more sophisticated maneuver is to have a friend call the reporter with the information. This leaves the would-be candidate even more room for denial.

To avoid being used in this way, check with other sources and see if it's possible the person can get money and a campaign organization together. It's not difficult to assess general chances.

Reporters with a "scoop" mentality are the ones most likely to succumb to trial balloons. If a reporter is "hot to get into print" as one of them put it, he runs everything he is told, whether it has substance or not.

Being Set Up

No doubt about it, reporters often get trapped by an informant. They are set up—that is, deliberately sandbagged with wrong information or else used to advance the informant's own position. Being set up sounds a bit like being lied to or floating a trial balloon, but it's more than that.

A reporter cannot always be positive he's been set up; instead a suspicion will surface and linger. "I've never been able to prove such a thing beyond doubt, but I am pretty sure I was. And I've become more cautious. You have to size people up. Some people have all the damned answers—no one has all the answers. I had a call the other day from a guy who said, 'I want you to come over here on this great story.' After a couple of questions, I knew in 30 seconds that he had nothing. There aren't too many who deliberately set you up. If he tells you something very self-serving, you can check it with other sources. I have never told a guy that he set me up the time before, and I always listen to him in the future because, hell, you never know when he might come up with something. He may give you nine bummers, but then come up with a good one."

A political reporter says a different tactic may be used in legislatures. "If a big thing is brewing and they don't want it known, they tell you another thing that sounds like it's big to get you to chase that other rabbit. This will keep you busy all day long and the next day you will learn about this other big story that they pulled over your eyes. It's a good ploy on their part. Depending on how well I know the guy who pulls it, I might let him know I am on to him. Sometimes you just let him think he got by with it and you get him the next time. If they pull this a lot, they lose credibility with you as a source, and they know it, so they sort of watch it.

"I even had one guy try to bribe me. He wanted to run for lieutenant governor and he wanted me to mention his name frequently in my political column. He offered to put me on a retainer. It was that blunt. He even told me that another reporter had done it. I didn't write about it or him; he ran for lieutenant governor and never really came out of the gate. Some guys say, 'Look, I'm going to run for governor or senator, and I want you to float some balloons and then I want you to be my news secretary.' It gets direct sometimes.''

Such tactics don't occur only with politicians. One man who was a reporter and editor on a national newspaper recalls his experience. ''There was a very technical story having to do with the Federal Reserve Board, when one of the issues was whether the FRB was going to change margin requirements for banks or something of this sort. I was covering the financial area: Treasury, Federal Reserve and so forth. I was told by an official that the FRB was not going to make any changes. He was in a position to know. He told me quite bluntly there was nothing going to be done. I wrote the story, which made the front page of my paper, and it was flat, 100 per cent wrong. He had deliberately misled me. I brought this up to him the next time I saw him. He said it was this kind of thing: Suppose you are a bank president and you know the bank is in trouble and you may have to close day after tomorrow. You don't go out and say this bank may have to close because, if you do, you precipitate the very thing you are trying to avoid. No President of the United States is going to say, 'The dollar will be devalued next week.' However, this FRB source did not have to lead me so far out of the way. He could have 'no-commented' or said, 'You know I can't talk about that,' rather than taken an overt act to mislead.''

Executive Sessions

The public's business is exactly that and should be conducted in the open; the public has the right to know. The press has no special right to be there; it is just there as a representative of the public that did not or could not attend. You are not covering a meeting for yourself or your paper or station, but for the public.

In many states, open meeting laws have been enacted by the legislatures to prevent closed-door sessions about the public business, except when those matters involve personnel or real estate proposals. However, governmental bodies still try to flip into executive session as soon as any potential difficulty arises in a meeting.

Reporters must know how to handle this situation because it necessitates the reporter's taking a stand. In this case a reporter becomes a part of his story, a development he tries to avoid under ordinary circumstances. But executive sessions aren't ordinary circumstances.

Executive sessions sometimes arise this way: There is a public meeting in progress, with reporters and perhaps members of the public on hand. At a pre-arranged point or when something potentially embarrassing arises, the chair will announce that the meeting is going into executive session.

At this point, the reporter should stay where he is. If necessary he should make the group move to another meeting place. If they claim, of course, that the meeting *is* being legally closed to the public, the reporter has no alternative but to leave. He can, however, report the circumstances under which he left.

One other way to handle this is to sit there and when asked to depart, ask the group to vote on ejecting you and other reporters. One veteran has done it this way. "When they say 'You'll have to leave,' I tell them 'No, you take a vote ejecting me and I will record who makes the motion and how the vote goes.' And then when I get outside the meeting I try to find out any way I can, like from a friendly source among the group, what went on and then I write a story about them holding a private meeting and also write what they discussed.

"If they say, 'We won't vote, get the hell out of here,' I don't go. I have a right to be there. I force them to call another meeting site, and then I show up again if I can find out about it. Sometimes in a session which is open, they say they are going into executive session and that reporters may stay if they agree to keep it off the record. I have never agreed to one of those things. I make them vote. I say 'I can't accept those conditions but I want to stay in the meeting.' And they say, 'We have to go into executive session to exclude you.' And I say, 'Okay, you vote in the public session to have the private session and to exclude the press' and then I do it the same way. But I make it part of the record that they voted to hold that meeting. I can't insure it's a roll call vote. In a big meeting you can't always get the names of who voted how if they move real fast. At a city council, a reporter can follow it and identify who voted which way. If you know the question will come up ahead of time, you can always get one council member to call for a division (those voting aye and nay have to stand in separate groups for their vote to be recorded). If they stand up, I can identify most of them. Or if another reporter will work with you, you split them. You take those that stand, or one-half the room. Two or three reporters can get it easily. I've done that, too.''

Rarely will this situation get to the point where a reporter is carried out bodily, but there have been cases at state legislatures where the sergeant-at-arms has been called to escort reporters out. When this occurs, write it.

While persisting in the call for open meetings and public action on public business, no reporter is naive enough to believe that council members, legislators, commissioners and such only discuss things after the gavel falls in the meeting. Of course, they get together privately and telephone each other. They often agree how they plan to vote. There is no way a reporter can prevent that. But a total blackout on public business can be prevented if reporters refuse to knuckle under.

An editor recalls how frustrating this can be. ''We began to be quite critical editorially of this government board which would jump into executive sessions to discuss personnel and land acquisition. That was allowed by law. But later on, from sources on the board, we would learn that the discussions had wandered to topics all over the map during this supposedly restricted session. We discovered this because we'd be talking to a source and he'd tell us things which we knew had never come out in news stories. I would ask, 'When was this discussed?' And the guy would say, 'It was discussed at the October meeting when we were in executive session.' The source, in this case, did not realize they were breaking the law by doing it. He just thought they got to talking about other things. But there's nothing a reporter can do about this. If you cover the open session of the meeting and the chair says 'We are now going into executive session to discuss real estate and personnel matters,' there's nothing you can do but get out.''

Threats

Threats against life and limb are very direct means of exercising news manipulation. In most cases threats are made to get a story or investigation halted. Threats can take two forms: against the news organization or against the reporter.

The threats against the firm generally run to ''I'll cancel all my advertising'' or ''Your building will be torched.'' The advertising threat is not a light one, particularly in small towns, where the pull-out of a major advertiser can be a serious financial problem. The reporter will not be in on this decision. It's up to the editor and publisher or the news director and general manager to decide if they are going to cave in.

Threats of physical harm to the plant are also dealt with by the ownership or managers, not by reporters.

The least worrisome threat against a reporter is ''I'll have you fired for this.'' True, it is a problem; the reporter is making waves; his boss may be annoyed at having to smooth ruffled feathers of some local bigwig; and an insecure reporter might be truly worried. But compared to physical violence, the loss of a job is nothing. The bombing death of an Arizona reporter was one of the relatively few cases where a journalist has been murdered by those opposed to his work. The threat of death, however, is not infrequent.

Some threatening phone calls have been answered by family members: ''I had written a front-page story about the Ku Klux Klan. One Saturday morning the phone rang and my young son answered. A voice said, 'If you want to see your Daddy again, you'd better tell him to lay off the Klan.' It upset him greatly. I thought about reporting it or pursuing it, but I just let it drop. I never heard anything else about it.''

''I've been threatened about someone suing me and the publisher,'' another recalls. ''Usually those things die down and nothing happens. In other cases, where a suit is filed, you just hope your editors are really behind you. I've had some people say they were going to come down and beat hell out of me. I have received 'breathing' phone calls at work and at home. No rocks through the windows, but I have had notes left on my windshield saying, 'If you don't keep your nose out of our business,' etc. In that case, I was looking at something involved with the local police department and police corruption.''

Another reporter recalls being followed. ''I was covering this political campaign and this very conservative nut would just follow me around. He followed me around at all the rallies and stuff, saying, 'I'm going to beat the hell out of you.' He was just this great big S.O.B., just everywhere I went.''

One reporter cited harassment. ''I got a rock through my windshield one time, and another time attended a voter registration meeting and came out to find someone had poured sand in my gas tank, or in Hertz's gas tank, I should say, and let the air out of the tires. During those days I would raise the hood occasionally to check against a bomb.''

Another reporter recalls his experience with threats and harrassment while a series ran. ''I got anonymous calls at the office, anonymous letters, too. At home for a number of months I would get midnight phone calls with just breathing, and I would cuss them out and still they wouldn't say anything. On one occasion two thugs came to my house. I wasn't at home that night and I'm not sure what would have happened if I had been there. My wife didn't tell them where I was because she could tell by looking at them they were thugs. On another occasion I had written some stories about kids whom the police caught drag racing. One night on my way home the guys stopped their machines in the middle of the road, trying to get me to stop my car. There were about six guys and obviously I didn't stop. They didn't try anything after that.''

Higher Reasons

Appealing to a reporter's sense of responsibility can be another form of manipulation.

One of the most far-reaching incidences of such manipulation involves the FBI. As exposés of the relationship between the FBI and reporters have shown, for decades the two have had what amounts to a partnership. Although reporters now question the propriety of working with the FBI rather than maintaining an objective stance, for years this symbiotic existence was encouraged. Both the FBI and the media were working for the public good, the reasoning went, so why not do it cooperatively?

As one author who has investigated the subject notes, "Somewhere along the way the FBI came to the decision to take advantage of the relationship, and certain segments of the press, whether wittingly or unwittingly, were had. So was the American public." (Paul Clancy, in *The Quill.*) Basically the FBI used its ability to offer reporters the inside story to ensure they would write that story the way the agency wished. J. Edgar Hoover's image was one of the primary beneficiaries of this type of power. Countless investigative reporters knew that if their stories did not present Hoover and the FBI as crusaders for the right then the source of those stories would be abruptly silenced.

Jack Anderson notes that when he took over Drew Pearson's "Washington Merry-Go-Round," Pearson had automatic clearance to files. But when Anderson started criticizing Hoover, the files slammed shut.

Even more complicated than the issue of whether to present the FBI accurately, however, was whether to cooperate with the bureau on stories concerning radicals and civil rights activists. In extreme instances reporters actually infiltrated organizations, reporting their findings to the FBI. In less extreme but equally distasteful circumstances, reporters were tools of propaganda issued by the FBI in efforts to discredit such outfits as the Black Panthers.

Although reporters now looking at these instances may feel that they would have been too clever to be involved, the issue becomes even more complex when we examine the civil rights movement.

As Clancy points out, "The first thing a reporter did upon arriving in a troubled southern town—after he made sure he wasn't being followed—was to find out where the 'feds' were . . ."

The feds tipped the reporters as to where the action was, and the reporters felt no qualms about giving the FBI any information they had, printable or unprintable. In this case, the "bad guys" seemed so clearly defined that anyone not willing to band together on the right side was no doubt forced to wonder if there were something missing in his moral makeup.

There are other times when a journalist comes across a good story or an interesting development and he is urged not to print it because, in effect, he will "mess things up" if he does. If he works in Washington, D.C., he may be told that reporting a given story will affect national security. If he works in a small town, he may be told his article will disrupt progress or start a riot. The manipulators try to appeal to the reporter on a "higher" level—asserting that in his position as wise seer, he should have the best interests of such-and-so at heart.

These decisions may be easy or difficult for the reporter and his bosses to resolve. There is no hard and fast rule for dealing with them. It is entirely possible that in Washington a reporter might come across something that would involve national security. *The New York Times* sat on the story about the proposed Bay of Pigs invasion; later, both President Kennedy and the *Times* management were to say it might better have been revealed so that plans could have been altered to prevent disaster. Of course, that is hindsight. Had the *Times* revealed the plans, the paper no doubt would have been castigated for undermining what might have been a highly successful mission.

In the Pentagon Papers matter, the government claimed "national security" but when the papers were released the information turned out to have been well-known. There is no question the government frequently slaps a "national security" defense on items that are merely politically embarrassing. Each instance must be weighed separately; the reporter must examine the import of the story and the credibility of his sources.

Government secrecy often reaches ludicrous levels. A television reporter did a feature story on a man who was selling 100,000 goldfish to the Commerce Department. The reporter called the department to ask the sale price and what the fish would be used for. The official would not answer, saying it was a private matter. When she threatened to use the Freedom of Information Act to dislodge the goldfish information, the official still wouldn't talk.

Local reporters also are implored not to write certain articles. If a journalist learns that a low-taxpaying, polluting industry is moving into town, he certainly should report it. But council members or state officials may want that industry so they can cite a broadened tax base and industrial growth. The citizens, however, may "nix" the idea if they learn of it in time. Government officials will tell the reporter he is standing in the way of progress, is doing a disservice to expansion, etc. and ask him to write nothing or to delay the story until the industry's plans are firm. But it is not for the reporter to decide that the people will or will not want the industry or that it should or should not be allowed. All he has to do is write that it's coming, its operational procedures and its history. Let the people decide what they want to do when they have the facts.

Another instance of keeping things from the public occurred in a city that was backing "scattered-site" public housing. Instead of putting low-income housing projects together in one area of the city, the federal government was encouraging development of public housing in all areas—including middle class and wealthy areas. The local housing authority refused to divulge the six sites. A television reporter called the regional office of Housing and Urban Development, learned the six locations and reported them. In this instance, the reporter was accused by housing authority members of trying to sabotage the project.

Reporters often find that officials don't mind media reporting of dams, new highways, housing projects, etc., but they want the stories *after* all papers have been signed, sealed and delivered. No doubt about it, many officials would frequently rather use reporters as "historians."

EN GARDE!

Reporters have always been leaned on. They tell what they know and that upsets people. Arguments and threats are overt and can be dealt with directly. Their perpetrators want you to know you are being intimidated; they want it blunt. But for the manipulator who practices his skill in devious ways, the game will be lost if the strategy is discovered.

One reporter says, "It's a battle. I don't say that occasionally a reporter doesn't fall off the line on the wrong side, and I wouldn't swear that there haven't been times when I or anyone else with some experience doesn't fall off. You just have to keep asking yourself, 'Am I serving this manipulator's selfish political interests or is there a public interest involved?' "

One editor sums up being used this way: "As far as being manipulated is concerned, the reporters deserve largely what they get, and if they are stupid enough to allow themselves to be manipulated, time after time, they deserve it. They have only themselves to blame."

Reporters may deserve it, but does the public?

A CASE HISTORY OF POLITICAL MANIPULATION

Since John F. Kennedy's presidential campaign, politicians and the public alike have become aware of the media-oriented campaign: the attempt to use the media so that a candidate gets the most benefit out of his press and broadcasting coverage. Several years ago, a media-oriented candidate mounted a gubernatorial primary campaign against a competitor who wouldn't or couldn't take advantage of the communication industry's shortcomings. The media-oriented candidate ultimately lost the general election, but in the process he abruptly educated the state's newspeople about modern campaigns. What follows are reminiscences of how the candidate played on journalism's weaknesses.

"The biggest, most flagrant example of manipulating the press occurred even before he paid his filing fee. He called what he billed as a 'major press conference' in the state's largest city. All the reporters trooped down there, and everyone thought 'This is it,' he will announce his candidacy for the gubernatorial race. Everyone was packed into the hotel meeting room, and he announced he was in favor of the current Washington administration, which happened to be his party. Everyone said 'Well, big deal,' and stormed out of there, just stomped out.

"It got to be a damned violent battle covering him. Ultimately the entire press corps turned on him. He very cleverly manipulated everyone. For instance, each of us would get a copy of his weekly schedule, laid out in advance. But we'd be going around with him and all of a sudden he'd say, like he just thought of it, 'We're going to so-and-so or such-and-such, instead, for a press conference.' But in the meantime, his folks in that town were calling up the local press, radio and television people to come over for a press conference—the spontaneity had all been carefully orchestrated. We'd get to the press conference site; he'd come in and read some statement giving his opponent hell for something. He'd pull this in the morning, about 11 or 12, not too much later than noon—so he gets to be on the 6 p.m. news, and it would be too late for the press traveling with the opponent to get film and fly it to the originating station as a rebuttal. So the other guy never got on film to respond: the station's anchorman just read the opponent's response. It was a damned clever ploy.

"He did this a couple times. And he'd declare 'No questions' before he read it, so that we didn't even get to pick at his statement. He just issued flat charges, no questions. One TV reporter tried to outfox him. When the candidate said, 'I've got this statement,' the reporter would ask, 'Are you going to answer questions afterward?' And when the candidate said no, this TV guy would turn off his lights, pack up his gear and walk out. Some of the others started following suit, and that ended that, but it went on for several weeks before it got stopped.

"He pulled another trick too. I had attended his speech in this little town one day but hadn't written anything on it as I was putting together another piece. The next day out on the road with him, I read our paper and it had a wire story that said he had said so-and-so and he hadn't said that at all, hadn't even come close. It turned out that his staff members, with his blessing, of course, were distributing press releases and saying he was making one speech when he really wasn't. But in good faith editors all over the state were running his news releases.

"Then a really funny thing happened. He went to one end of the state and said, 'If we need more revenue, I won't hesitate to put a tax on tobacco.' This comment was duly reported. But he went down east where the crop is grown a few days later and called the news report a damned lie, saying he would never tax tobacco. But it just so happened that at the first speech a radio reporter had taped what he said and hadn't gotten around to erasing it yet. And the guy produced the speech and the candidate was caught. After that, all of us carried tape recorders because it was plain to see the guy would flat-out lie and discredit your report—even though lots of other people had heard him say those original words. He was playing quite a game. It took him, surprisingly, a long time to learn that what you say in one part of the state nowadays—or in the country or world for that matter—is going to get reported elsewhere the same day.

"He also tried going to one part of the state and saying he was for the President, and going elsewhere in the state and saying he really did like ol' George Wallace. In one place he was the party loyalist where it was demanded; in the other part he was hedging because he knew Wallace had a good hold on the voters.

"It must be remembered, too, that while all this was going on, he kept accusing us journalists of mistreating him and quoting him out of context and all the rest.

"He also got close to provoking dangerous situations for some of us reporters. One time we followed him through a section of Klan country. We pulled up to a service station at the same time as a lot of pickup trucks with gun racks in them. He was down on the press at that time, and he said to the group, 'Look here, boys, what I've got with me, the reporter from such-and-such newspaper.' Now we are a pretty liberal newspaper to begin with. And I tell you the truth, that was a scary situation. He was doing it to be vindictive, and wanted to embarrass me, which he did. One of the guys said, 'Oh, is that so? We'd rather talk to him than talk to you.' Fortunately, nothing came of it, but I slumped down a little further in my seat and I didn't appreciate it at all, to tell you the truth.

"He also lied directly to us. We wound up in this one city on a Friday during the campaign. We hit several mill shifts and stuff, and it had been a long week and everyone was tired. We were happy he was cutting his schedule short and going home. He told us during lunch, 'This is it, boys. My daughter has a birthday today, so I'm going home, got a cake for her and just going to make a little family gathering of it.' Fine, we were all overjoyed. I was tired and for a change I got home fairly early. Everyone had taken off on his separate way, except for two fellows from another paper. They didn't believe him. They followed him in their car, and he did not go home. He went to a cabin in an eastern county and met with some of the local leaders of his party—leaders who were supposed to be on the outs with him. It was a fence-mending proposition. They wrote it up into a nice story. One of the reporters got onto it because somebody in the campaign misspoke himself earlier in the day and indicated to the reporter that the boss was going to this county. So they didn't take the birthday party bit at face value. When they tracked him to this town they inquired at a local filling station where the meeting was on his behalf, and lo and behold, there he was.

"Being evasive is one thing; all the press was used to that. But this was flat-out lying. He did it another time, at least.

"In another county we were all holed up in the local motel. His aide told us the candidate was going to take a nap, that nothing was scheduled all afternoon; he was just going to rest up. The aide told us that we could be filing stories or drinking or whatever we wanted, that we had so much free time. So we were all doing different things when someone noticed that the man's car was gone. We found the aide, who said 'Yeah, something came up and he had to leave.' We found out later he had had a secret meeting with some Indians to try to get their support. But in the meantime, when he returned, we all pounced on him. 'Where the hell have you been? Why did you tell us you were going to take a nap? Why've you been taking off and leaving us stranded at this motel?' We had come in an airplane and didn't even have a car with us, which he knew. That added to our anger. And this candidate just jumps on his aide and says, 'I told you to get these guys a car. Why didn't you get them a rental car? You were supposed to do that.' The aide was just his fall guy; I felt sorry for him after it was all over. But the aide tells him there's just one damn rental car in this town and that had been taken. So the candidate contacts one of his supporters and tells us, 'All right, we're going out to visit service stations and stuff around the county and you can use the local party chairman's car to follow us in.' And then they played this swell game of trying to lose us on the road.

"In the meantime, we had been reporting the appearance of bumper stickers showing this candidate, with Wallace pictured on them too. They just showed up in this one part of the state where Wallace was really strong. But the candidate and Wallace both denied knowing anything about where the stickers came from or who was distributing them. Across the front of the lead car in this procession was a big poster saying 'This candidate for governor.' The poster started flapping and they pulled into this gas station to tie it back down. We pulled in behind them and we saw that underneath on the car's bumper were these Candidate/Wallace bumper stickers that everyone had denied knowing about. For our benefit they had taped them over. One of the campaign supporters tried to stand in such a way to block our seeing it, but it was too late.

"One of the TV guys had had his gear stowed in the local party chairman's car trunk by the chairman, who was driving. He asked to get it, to film some of this and he walked back with the chairman to the trunk. The lid went up and inside, under the tripods and lights and stuff, were all these leaflets, bumper stickers and other materials linking Wallace and this candidate. Right in the back of the local chairman's car, but everyone was denying it. So that just exposed hell out of his attempt to manipulate one part of the state into believing one thing about him, while he was soft-pedaling it elsewhere. And if that wasn't enough, at the next stop, one of his local people was already passing these folders out to the crowd! So we reported what we saw.

"But they still played revenge, because by this time the candidate was really playing 'Fight the Press.' They had a rally that night and afterwards said they had some private meetings, but that they were turning us over to their local supporters who would take us to a private club where we could get a drink, the only place in this town. We welcomed the idea and we arranged to meet the campaign crew at the local airport around midnight to fly back to the capital. But when we arrived at the airport, we found out that the candidate and his staff had gone, taken both planes and just left us stranded out there and the local airport wasn't even open at that hour. He was trying to get us all so mad that we would write just totally slanted stuff and then he could say so. That's what it amounted to.

"I wouldn't want to get in a battle between the print and broadcast media but at least the print media has time to reflect a little on what they're doing. In dealing with this guy, if he made an announcement and wouldn't answer questions I didn't consider that a press conference and considered it no more than a routine hand-out, a press statement. But he wasn't playing to the press, he was playing to TV which needs sound-on-film. I have shown up at other press conferences, or so-called press conferences, they are really created events, and never written a word out of them. I always try to ask questions, and I report if he held a 'press conference' and that he wouldn't answer. You become a victim in a sense because you must show up for the things because competitors show up.

"With this guy, I don't think the state's press or broadcast media were ready for him. He was the first to put on a media-oriented campaign. Before we got through the issue got to be what kind of campaign he was running; how he hid out from the campaign; how he lied. It was at one of these 'press conferences' that the reporters' scales started tipping against him. He lied about the role of one of his aides, even though 90 per cent of the reporters in the room knew the answer to the question before it was answered—but he lied even though he knew all the reporters knew otherwise."

As mentioned earlier, this manipulative candidate lost. Not all do.

8

Of Pots and Kettles:
Ethics for the Investigative Reporter

---

*"Violating the law should not be done
casually . . . it should only be done soberly,
advisedly, and in the fear of God."*

Journalists usually know a lot about ethics—everyone
else's.

When it comes to exposing the misdeeds of someone else,
the reporter generally has no qualms. After all, the newsman
reasons, the guy's guilty, isn't he?

Yet when his own conduct is at issue, the working reporter
often has no clearly formulated set of principles. The American
Society of Newspaper Editors has compiled a list of the canons
of journalism. While the canons provide admirable goals of behavior, journalistic ethics, like all ethics, inevitably comes
down to a matter of personal beliefs and, to a certain degree, to
the situation at hand. Newsmen should anticipate likely ethical
problems and formulate a position in these areas before actually
being called upon to act. At the moment of on-the-spot decision, cool reason is normally the first casualty.

Reportorial Arrogance

To be a reporter is to hold power. No matter how the reporter exercises that power, he still makes people uneasy when

he calls for information. To write about a subject from any point of view is to lift it out of the ordinary.

Ironically, many newsmen have preferred to see themselves as mere transmitters of the news—funnels through which the material was channeled. They perceived themselves as lacking responsibility for what they transmitted; their only function was to ensure that the information they conducted was as accurate and complete as possible. Yet the power vested in the reporter—to embarrass, ridicule, shape events, even to destroy—means that he always does much more than serve as a conduit. This is the case even when the journalist is not indulging in the one-sided reporting that is termed "advocacy journalism."

We have explored in earlier chapters the criteria used by journalists in deciding to pursue and publicize one story while deciding to ignore another. The reporter must consciously and conscientiously examine why he selects certain stories and how he subsequently treats them.

A cavalier attitude of "let the chips fall where they may" is sometimes an acceptable response, depending on the story. But that attitude must be tempered with responsibility. Rooting out the truth is done not only to get a story but to ensure that you're not unjustifiably ruining a person's reputation. Unfair and unfounded stories can damage a person's job, his entire career or home life.

Arrogance of power is never a pleasant sight, and newspeople must be particularly vigilant that they don't become self-righteous, feeling their cause excuses any and all behavior, methods or conclusions, no matter how outrageous.

Arrogance may be manifested by doing half a job. Covering the surface of the news, superficially telling the public what occurred without seeking deeper reasons, is in itself amoral. For the reporter, laziness, lack of preparation or a half-job can have consequences too broad to be dismissed as unimportant. Thus, the reporter should see himself not as a transmitter, but as a microscope of the events he covers. His work in uncovering the facts magnifies and reveals the true story. The reporter's ethical duty is to pursue and document the complete situation.

Conflicts of Interest

Just as the politician can be guilty of a conflict of interest in voting on a proposal in which he has a personal stake, a reporter may also, sometimes quite casually, find himself in a situation where his own bank account or reputation stands to gain or suffer.

The most common category of such a situation involves the "freebie." For example, women's page staffers are deluged with cosmetics each time a company introduces a new product. Fashion writers find themselves offered a new handbag when a famous designer enters the popular market. Business editors get offers of products from the companies about which they write. Trucking industry lobbyists sponsor weekly buffets, inviting media members to indulge themselves in beef and booze. The mayor hands the city hall reporter tickets to a sold-out concert. Can Madame Editor wear a "freebie" brand of cosmetics and then easily write an exposé of how that company's other products are a health hazard? Can the business editor smoke cartons of free cigarettes and then truthfully explore the shady side of the manufacturer's bookkeeping practices? Firms will continue to press gifts and champagne parties upon willing reporters, as long as it's "good business."

Along the same line, but more harmless, are the gifts which are spontaneously and innocently offered and spontaneously and innocently received. A woman queried as a minor source in an investigative story may give the newsman some tomatoes from her garden. She is hardly trying to influence the article; nor does the reporter feel his integrity is being damaged. If a few tomatoes are accepted, then does one go on to accept a $5 lunch from someone else? Then does one also say okay to $10 tickets to a college football game? It's only a matter of degree from there to television sets, weekend jaunts, crates of liquor at Christmas. Just where do you draw the line? That is up to the individual reporter and he'd best judge the source of the gift, its motivation, its worth and what an enemy could make of the situation. As he will soon learn, things are often not illegal or immoral but may nevertheless suggest impropriety.

To avoid "looking bad," many news organizations have stringent rules against these gratuities, but others permit the reporter to make his own decisions. Even if the reporter denies that a few gifts are able to win his favor, are these same gifts worth risking the appearance of bias? When he writes a trucking industry article, or one analyzing the mayor's proposals, would his work have credibility if his readers knew of the free dinners or gifts? While common sense and courtesy must prevail, a reporter must be alert to suggestions of conflicts of interest.

More invidious than the usual freebies are the junkets which entertainment editors, sports writers, food editors and travel writers often accept from the subjects of their articles. The same newspaper which prohibits its reporters from accepting a Christmas ham will allow the travel editor to fly to Bermuda on an all-expense-paid trip, stay in a new hotel and return to write an "objective" account of its facilities. For entertainment editors, movie studios and television networks finance posh visits to California or to the location of a new film. Reporters who do not write flattering accounts are seldom, if ever, invited for a second visit. The small amount of investigative reporting in these fields is hardly surprising when one considers the source of most of such "news." The food editor's reading or listening audience never knows that the flour company indirectly paid plenty for the clutch of stories about its Chocolate Cake Cook-off winner. And, if there is something wrong with the flour company, the public usually will never learn that either.

Harrison Salisbury's involvement with Xerox Corporation is an example of potential conflict of interest. Salisbury was the author of an article Xerox commissioned and "sponsored" for *Esquire*. Supposedly, *Esquire* had the right to reject the article, but its publication was indirectly tied in with advertisements the corporation was also purchasing in the magazine. Critics queried both author's and editor's objectivity. Eventually Xerox, after mulling over the pros and cons of the idea, decided not to pursue similar projects.

Moonlighting is another area in which the reporter can find himself compromising his integrity. Politicians and businessmen need speeches and news releases; hospitals need newsletters; government agencies need reports summarized. Many of them do not have full-time aides to handle such tasks. The friendly local reporter is asked to help out—for a fee, of course.

The newsman can find himself doing such work because he does not consider its possibilities. The editor of a weekly newspaper, for example, constantly berated the governor of his state on the editorial page; simultaneously, he was helping to compose the governor's speeches. Perhaps he felt there was no conflict because he was not praising the official; perhaps he did not think.

"I was covering the legislature," says one newswoman, "when one of the members asked me to write releases for his hometown paper. Naturally I would have known it was unethical to accept money for trying to get something in my own paper for him. But writing them for his paper seemed innocent enough, so I accepted. Later it dawned on me that I was still in debt to him; that it might appear I would hesitate to write something unflattering about him for my own paper since he was, in a sense, my 'boss.' Such a problem never arose, yet it easily could have. And when I thought the matter over, I realized how naive I had been."

Still another reporter might be accused of a conflict of interest because he influenced the actions of a public official in order to get a story. Later he questioned his own ethics. "The mayor of our city owns a department store chain, and he threw his nephew out of one of their board meetings. The nephew decided to sue the mayor for assault, and he went to a magistrate to seek a warrant against the mayor. The magistrate, who has discretionary authority in such cases, said he would sleep on it before making a decision. The nephew called us and told us what had happened and what he intended to do. We called the magistrate to confirm it and he said he might not sign it after all. He said he had to think about it.

"We said, 'Well, we might be out that way soon, how about letting us look at what might be drawn up, see what it says and when you sign it we'll have the story ready and we won't have to call you again. We can check back on Monday to see what you decided to do.' The magistrate agreed and we got the details. But we also told him, 'Well, we guess if you don't sign it a whole lot of people will think you didn't because it was the mayor who was involved. We know it's not true, but people will think that.' We talked to him for a long time and got him to sign the thing in time for our paper's deadline, so the competing afternoon paper had to scrounge around for other angles.''

INVASION OF PRIVACY

Reporters invade the privacy of their subjects every day. That's the nature of the job. Except in cases of libel and in very specific areas where privacy becomes a legal matter, however, only the reporter himself decides exactly how far he will go in attempting to learn all.

Invasion by Questions

The reporter who finds himself calling the mother of a child lost in the mountains to ask, "Is he afraid of the dark?" may do well to ask what purpose is being served. The journalist who writes a Christmas Eve piece about a child who choked to death on a tree ornament and is then ordered by the desk to "Call back and find out what color the ornament was" may also wonder whether the public's right to know is being purchased too dearly. People devastated by tragedy have had microphones shoved in their faces by callous broadcast newsmen who inquire, "And how did it feel, Mr. Jones, when you learned both your children died in the blaze?" As one reporter notes, "I'm always surprised when they don't reply, 'Go to hell.' ''

The ethical question here is whether the reporter becomes the instrument of an unethical goal. Does he seek news which will make his story well-read without considering the effect the piece will have on those it concerns? When the subject of a story is viewed as a monster whose deeds make him deserve whatever he gets, that question may seem easy enough to answer. But do the children of such a person deserve to be pursued and questioned on the way home from school; should the wife be hassled on her way to the supermarket? And, in those instances where the newsmaker is such only by the workings of fate, can we justify the picking, prodding and compiling of ghoulish or personal details which make the reader gasp but which remove the last shred of dignity from the subject?

Reporters reason that they are justified in such invasions because their colleagues take similar measures or because their editors stonily make such assignments. The acceptable stance, however, is that the reporter ask such questions only when he is convinced that they are vital to presenting a story which needs to be told.

When asking questions, reporters sometimes omit the fact they are reporters. But they frequently draw the line at misrepresenting themselves, particularly as certain figures.

"I think it is okay to impersonate people who don't have the authority to compel information," says one investigative reporter. "I wouldn't impersonate a policeman, lawyer or doctor. I would say 'I am taking a survey and wonder if this is the house of Joe Jones.' But I wouldn't go up and say, 'I am a detective. Is this Joe Jones' house?' "

Invasion by a Side Door

Victims of tactless questions at least know they are being attacked; victims of another sort of reportorial tactic quite often are taken unaware.

Reporters will bend ethics to suit them. For example, one reporter recalls, "We asked for the Parole Board file on this felon, and fortunately the guy we asked didn't know that we shouldn't have been given the file. There are aspects of these files that are public information and then there are aspects that aren't. The guy gave us the entire file. And then he left the room. I knew he was ignorant of the regulations, but I wasn't going to tell him. We had full access to everything. And we copied it all down. Based on this file we interviewed some people and got a series of stories together that ran over a period of weeks." Reporters are not renowned for giving a sucker an even break.

Snooping may produce results that are only harmless and merely sophomoric; however, it can lead in graduated steps to actually breaking the law. Here, too, the reporter must be aware of the consequences. He may choose to totally commit himself to pursuit of the facts, but he must not make the commitment casually.

"One of the things I learned to do, and can still do to some extent, is to read a letter upside down," says a veteran discussing a common journalistic trick. "You stand looking at a man's desk and try to read a letter while you are talking to him or waiting for him to get off the phone. Ninety per cent of the time what you read doesn't do you any good at all, but it's good practice, a lot of fun and, once in a while, you get a clue to something."

"I remember a case," says another, "where I was trying very hard to get a story from a guy who just wouldn't tell me. So I asked him questions, and we talked about all sorts of things. And I'd get up and stroll around the room, talk and ask questions and put the note pad down and walk around the room some more. And, finally, I ended up behind his desk and he swung around in his chair to talk to me. And I was reading what was on his desk."

Such antics hardly seem reprehensible although they do violate the traditional gentleman's concept of honor. But many reporters feel that when news is right there before their eyes, dedication to their jobs requires them to take a look—even if it's upside down or over someone's shoulder.

Going a step further, however, causes most of them to hesitate. They do not shuffle quite so casually through a man's papers or open desk drawers and peek inside, yet some confess to having done so when they felt a situation demanded action.

One newsman openly admits to having gone through wastebaskets in search of abandoned drafts, yet says, "Well, it's unethical to go through any private person's effects, but this would have a lot to do with what you are after. If you've got a public official particularly, and you think he's a crook, and he's stealing from the public till, I wouldn't draw the line very tightly. . . . Yes, if I were convinced the man was a crook, and it was just a matter of getting the evidence, then I might. . . . I don't advise other reporters to do this. I think this is a determination that has to be made by the reporter on the spot. If I were an editor and a guy came in with something that I knew had been taken from the city manager's desk, or what not, I would say, 'Don't tell me where you got this.' "

Another reporter points out that sometimes people expect you to examine their papers. "An old trick of the trade," he says, "is when a man wants you to know things but doesn't want to tell you, he says, 'You know, I've got to go to the bathroom,' and he reaches down in his files and picks something out and puts the sheets he wants you to see on his desk and says, 'I'll be back in about 15 minutes.' "

The humorist, H. Allen Smith, wrote a hilarious account of such an experience in *To Hell in a Handbasket*. He was working for the *Louisville Times* when he was sent to Camp Knox.

National Guard units from Kentucky, Indiana, and West Virginia were in training at Camp Knox, a big military establishment thirty miles from Louisville. . . . This is the same place that later changed its name to Fort Knox and got all that gold. Mr. Aronson sent me down to Camp Knox to represent both the *Times* and the *Courier-Journal*. I was given a comfortable room in a cottage occupied by two officers; I was permitted to eat at the officers' mess; and I had free run of the entire camp, possibly because I was the only reporter present.

During my stay in Camp Knox I was responsible for the biggest political story to break in recent Kentucky history—a scandal that had wide repercussions, reaching even to the floor of the United States Senate. It involved the Adjutant General of Kentucky and through him the Governor and a lot of other statesmen. To the best of my recollections there were two warring factions—the Governor and his adherents, and another group bent upon throwing the incumbent rascals out. Let me make it clear—I didn't know a single thing about this political war at the time the story broke. I don't know anything about it to this day. I was at Camp Knox writing long dispatches back to my paper about the sham warfare between the Red Forces and the Blue Forces and who was winning and what new units were coming in from Breathitt County and Lieutenant So-and-so from Paducah fell off a horse and broke his leg.

One day an orderly came to see me and said that General Such-and-such wanted to see me in his office. This General was a

Louisville financier and politician, one of the leaders of the group opposed to the Governor. I walked into his office and he waved me into a seat and then gave me a sheet of paper with some chitchat regarding certain minor promotions in his command. I was glancing through it when he said:

"See this document right there?" He indicated a sheaf of papers lying on his desk. "This document involves a secret matter and if I should be called away from this office, you are not to look at it. Understand?"

"Oh, yes sir!" I assured him.

"It is a document," he went on, tapping on it with his forefinger, "of great political importance. If its contents became known to the public it would shake the State of Kentucky to its very foundations. Therefore, nobody must see it unless they are authorized to see it. Most of all, you newspaper reporters. I want it clearly understood, no newspaper reporter is to see this document. IS THAT CLEAR?"

"Oh, yes sir!" I exclaimed with great sincerity. Why should he doubt me, I wondered? My God, I was a trustworthy person, a person of integrity. I wouldn't have dreamed of . . .

"Every newspaper in the state," the General went on, "and especially the newspapers in Louisville, and most especially the *Courier-Journal* and *Times,* those papers would give their eye-teeth to get their hands on this document. I tell you, it's a political bombshell. A po-litical buh-omb-shell! It's so . . ."

The telephone on his desk rang, he answered it, listened a moment, then said he'd be right over. He got up from the desk, tapped his finger again on the forbidden document and once again uttered his warning.

"I have to leave this office," he said. "I'll be gone at least half an hour. Now, remember—you . . . are . . . not . . . to . . . look . . . at . . . this . . . document!"

"Don't you worry, General." I said, getting up. "I wouldn't dream of even touching it." I started briskly for the door. People don't have to say things twice to me.

"Don't leave," he told me. "You can loaf in here till I get back. There's some booze in that cabinet over there. Help yourself. But remember what I said—don't go reading that document! Don't read it!" Now there was a big grin on his face, and he was jerking his head in the direction of his desk, and then he contorted his face into a monstrous wink, and then he winked again, and then a third time. After that he left. I stood there a moment in deep thought. Suddenly it came to me. "Say!" I spoke aloud. "I do believe that he wants me to have a look at that document." I approached it nervously, cautiously, as if it were a venomous snake. I wasn't too sure of my ground and I wouldn't have been surprised if grim-visaged troopers with Lugers at the ready had come swarming through the windows. But I got hold of my apprehensions and read the beginning of the document and recognized what it was. They were bringing serious charges against the Adjutant General and making grave and nasty charges against the government in Frankfort. I decided to risk all, including my life, and made notes as fast as I could, and then hurried out and found a telephone and called Mr. Aronson at the *Times*. I told him that I wasn't sure about the General's intentions, that he might have been perfectly sincere in telling me not to touch the document, and I think that Mr. Aronson used the name of the Lord. He told me to read my notes to a rewrite man and then to stay where I was until reinforcements arrived.

Within an hour it began to rain reporters at Camp Knox. I remember that the old pro, Howard Hartley, arrived on the run and gave me a pat on the back and a big grin and said, "Quite a scoop, boy!" The important journalists from my own papers pushed me to one side, ignoring the fact that I was responsible for the whole thing. I had pictured myself in the role of hero, but to those guys I was just a jerk cub. I wasn't too unhappy about it when, a couple of days later, I was ordered back to Louisville.

That is the true story of my great journalistic coup at Camp Knox. It proves, once again, the enduring value of the tried-and-true principles. In the newspaper game it is necessary that a man be always alert; let him keep his mind ever clear, let him stand to the main chance, let him know the motives of men, and interpret them correctly. I know whereof I speak. I have been through the cauldron!

The Watergate investigation by *The Washington Post* raised a number of similar privacy issues. Reporters on the case later admitted they were clearly guilty of obtaining information via methods which the government had been criticized for using. They sought sources within telephone and credit card companies, for example, to ascertain telephone calls, restaurant and hotel bills, airline ticket purchases, etc. This information was private, and had the reporters themselves been subjected to such scrutiny, they say, they would have felt their constitutional rights had been violated.

For newsmen involved in such major investigations, the intricacies of obtaining tightly held material may lead them to go even further, to actually break the law.

An editor says, "I confess to very queasy feelings about the use of stolen material and this sort of thing, about a reporter violating the law in order to do something. Yet I am willing to say that under certain circumstances and at certain times I might do it myself. If I may draw a rather broad analogy, I do not believe in murder. I believe in the commandment, 'Thou shall not kill.' But I can easily conceive a situation where I would kill someone without a qualm afterwards. Now I might do it and justify it on that particular thing, if the man were attacking me or my wife, or something of this sort. But I wouldn't take the second step of saying that because I did it in this particular case, therefore the commandment against murder is not valid. Generally speaking, I think a reporter ought to ask himself 'Is what I am doing really justifying my violating the law or some ethical principle?' It should not be done casually. It should be done only soberly, advisedly and in the fear of God."

Inevitably if a newsman rationalizes what he does in an "ends justify the means" claim, he finds himself in the same position as many of the people he is accusing. "The reporter has to ask himself if, in order to get this S.O.B. who's a crook, does he himself become a crook? I think it is a nice question. And I think the reporter ought to pause and ask himself that. What is the difference between breaking and entering to get a good story and breaking and entering to find out that someone's a traitor? It's still breaking and entering. Theft is theft, and it doesn't cease to be theft because the thief happens to be a newspaper reporter," the editor adds.

One reporter got his story by breaking into a sheriff's desk drawer, but he also got arrested himself. An editor recounts the story. "This fellow broke open the sheriff's drawer to get these checks out. They Xeroxed them and then put all the checks back in the drawer. The paper pounced on the sheriff's department, and the sheriff's department had breaking and entering charges filed against the reporter and the newspaper, of which they were really guilty and had admitted as much, but the sheriff at the same time was taking payoffs from half the people in the county and the whole sheriff's department was fired. When the charges against the reporter and the newspaper were brought before the grand jury, they were immediately quashed.''

Depending on the investigative piece, reporters have to weigh the risks of their actions. In these days of electronics, it is inevitable, of course, that the investigative reporter is faced with the option of going a step further in his snooping. "Bold Enough to Get Wired?'' questions an article in *More*. Outfitting yourself with such helpful goodies as cufflink microphones designed to bug unsuspecting sources raises ethical questions which didn't arise in previous generations.

Encouraging others to break the law, or benefiting when they do so, raises other ethical points. Use of the Pentagon Papers and Woodward and Bernstein's attempt to question members of the Watergate Grand Jury are examples. Although it was not illegal for reporters to question jury members, it would have been illegal for the jurors to reply, and Woodward and Bernstein admit to having chosen "expediency over principle'' by soliciting the information.

There are two yardsticks reporters seem to use when determining how far they will pursue knowledge: 1) the importance of the issue and 2) whether the people involved are private citizens or public officials. The more significant the story's impact and the more public the figure involved, the greater the tendency to follow the reporter's instinct all the way.

There are reporters who feel they must be above reproach to make their stories undiminished by their own actions. "I have always taken this approach,'' says one veteran investigative reporter. "If you are after somebody about a violation of the law or unethical conduct, you have to keep clean yourself. You shouldn't taint your own evidence by doing anything illegal or unethical. The cleaner you can go in, the better.''

A CASE HISTORY OF LAWBREAKING

Following is the account of how two reporters broke into a room in a county courthouse to get information on election fraud. Their actions can lead to many questions of ethics: Are they not as guilty of crime as their subjects? Does their end justify their means? If news organizations break the law to get what they need and/or want, can they rant editorially against such tactics by government?

Here are the reporters' descriptions of their actions:

"After each election there was always a story out of the mountain counties in which the losing faction was charging the winners with fraud connected with absentee ballots. The allegations went on year after year. We finally just decided that where there was so much smoke, there must be some fire and that if we spent enough time and knew what we were doing, we could show whether this was true or not.

"Our tip in this case was simply the accumulated stories in the paper. We did enough telephoning and talking with political people so that we were convinced the story was there. The only doubt we had was how much we could document and whether we could get something done about it since there was an entrenched political opposition to any changes in the law. We read the law thoroughly, and we knew that we could get at certain kinds of records without going to these mountain counties first. The law required that duplicates of certain records kept in the county had to go to the state level. We knew where the majority of the complaints had come from, so we simply went to the state elections board office, pulled duplicates and got innumerable leads right there. They were available to anyone who wanted to go in and look at them and on their faces they were violations of the law. For instance, we found applications or absentee ballots that were issued in the name of a neighbor—spelled N-a-b-o-r—which was a clear violation of the law. No one had any idea who had those ballots. It could have been anyone who walked in off the street.

"As I recall, we spent six to ten weeks on the story, and during that time they held elections in one of the counties.

There were some charges made, and we went to the county to look at the records.

"The courthouse in this sparsely populated county served several functions. On the first floor was the public library. There were the usual courtrooms. And the sheriff's office was head-quartered there too.

"The officials had impounded the records in this little courthouse—the ballot boxes were stacked in a storage room under a stairway. They said they were soon going to move the boxes to a local bank vault 'for safekeeping.' Knowing the history of the county and the people involved, we knew damn well that if those records were kept there, that before they got into the proper investigative hands, some of them were going to disappear or get mutilated or something. We decided to have a look at those records despite the fact that they were locked in that room."

The other reporter who worked on the story continues: "The courthouse had closed for business and we just didn't leave. It had to stay open because the sheriff's office was there, and the exterior doors had to be unlocked. All interior offices were locked. We just started wandering around, quietly. There was a little closet-like door and stairs going to a cupola on top. That little storage room had a type lock on it which is very easy to flip back with a pocketknife or pin or such. God, I was sweating. My colleague stood guard, and I went into the room. There were the ballot boxes.

"I had a note pad and I wrote down the count and how they looked physically. One box with red tape across, another with three strips this way, another box so-and-so. Got a physical description down to a knothole in one of them. And we were there maybe 15 minutes. He was looking out, and I could hardly hold my pencil because if we were caught, we'd be in jail. I finally finished and we got out. We didn't get the boxes themselves; they were locked.

"We called the State Board of Elections chairman and we said 'Damn it, we have reason to believe that if those boxes are left here over the weekend, there won't be any case by Monday. We want state authorities in here now.' But they couldn't get the investigators in that day. Monday morning they arrived and they supervised the transfer of the boxes from the courthouse into the vault at the savings and loan across the street. And when they were pulled out and I compared them to the description I had written down, they weren't the same. From Saturday afternoon when we had broken into that room and looked at them, until Monday when they transferred them, those boxes had been gone into and some had been tampered with. We didn't say in our story that we too had broken in. But we did print physical descriptions of the boxes before and after. That's one time I blew my cool and acted like a Hollywood reporter. We had fun on that one.''

Their story led to a legislative revision of absentee ballot laws.

Index

Adams, Samuel Hopkins, 9
Advocacy journalism, 128
Alcoholism, in reportable story, 85-88
All the King's Men (Warren), 90
All the President's Men (Bernstein and Woodward), 4, 64
Almond, Lindsay, 23
American Heritage, 15
American Magazine, The, 8
American Medical Association dictionary, 53
American Society of Newspaper Editors, 127
Anderson, Jack, 6, 24, 88, 89, 118
Anderson, Paul Y., 9
Arrogance, reportorial, 127-28
Association experts, as sources for investigative reporting, 49-50

Background sources, 76
Baker, Ray Stannard, 8
Bay of Pigs invasion, 119
Beat: people on, as sources of information, 42-44; story ideas found on, 22-24
Bernstein, Carl, 1, 7, 23, 45, 52, 63, 139
Black Panthers, 118
Bohlen, Charles, 15

Bok, Edward, 9
Boys on the Bus, The (Crouse), 47
Boys' Town, probe of, 34, 37-40
Bribe, difficulty of pinning down, 94-95, 99
Buffett, Warren, 37

Canons, of journalism, 127
Carter, Jimmy, 108, 111
Case histories: of abandoned stories, 96-101; on controlling situation, 79-82; of lawbreaking by reporters, 140-42; of political manipulation, 121-26; of real stories initially ignored, 33-40; on source finding, 54-58
Central Pacific Railroad, and *Sacramento Union*, 8
Chappaquidick, 88
Charlotte Observer, The, 27
City councils, 115
Civil rights movement, 118
Clancy, Paul, 118
Collier's magazine, 8, 9
Columbia Journalism Review, 33, 53, 109
Commerce Department, U.S., 119
Conference, news, 105-06
Conflicts of interest, and ethics for reporter, 129-32

143

Control of situation, 76-82; case history on, 79-82
Crouse, Timothy, 47
Cuban missile crisis, 45

Davis, Richard Harding, 15; quoted, 15-16
Dean, John, 26
Deep background sources, 76
"Deep Throat," 45
Detroit News, The, 85
Dictionary, American Medical Association, 53
Dun and Bradstreet, 52

Eagleton, Thomas, 88
Encyclopedia of Associations, 49
Esquire magazine, 34, 130
Ethics for investigative reporter, 127-42 *passim;* and conflicts of interest, 129-32; and moonlighting, 130-31; *see also* Invasion of privacy; Lawbreaking by reporter
Everybody's Magazine, 9
Executive sessions, 113-16

Fairness, importance of, 59-61
Families of officials, and reportable stories, 89-90
Father Flanagan's Boys' Home, probe of, 34, 37-40
Federal agents, working with, 78-79
Federal Bureau of Investigation (FBI), 79, 117-19
Federal Reserve Board, 113
Files, reporter's, as source for stories, 30-31, 53-54

Finding Facts (Rivers), 52
Flanagan, Edward J., 37
Ford, Gerald R., 108
Fox, Fanne, 85
"Freebies," 129-30
Freedom of Information Act, 54, 120

General Accounting Office, 52
Goldwater, Barry, 17
Government officials, working with, 78-79
Great Depression, 9

Hamilton, Alexander, 8
Harding, Warren G., 9
Hays, Wayne, 24, 85
Health, Education and Welfare, Department of, 52
Hendrick, Burton J., 8
Hersh, Seymour, 9
Hoover, J. Edgar, 118
Housing and Urban Development, Department of, 52, 120
How to Find the Law (Roalfe, ed.), 53

Internal Revenue Service (IRS), 39, 79
Interview: beginning, 66-67; controlling, 63-76; and identification of reporter, 65-66; and liar, handling, 71-73; and listening to answers, 70-71; and microphone, keeping, 73-74; obtaining, 63-65; off-the-record, 74-76; questions asked during, 67-70
Intuition, and investigative reporting, 28-30

Invasion of privacy, 132-39; by questions, 132-33; by side door, 133-39
Investigative reporting, 2-12; and association experts, 49-50; and beat, *see* Beat; and characteristics of reporter, 13-20; and control of situation, *see* Control of situation; cumulative effect of, 7, 11; defined, 2-3; documentation for, 90*ff.;* ethics for, *see* Ethics for investigative reporter; files, reporter's, as source for, 30-31, 53-54; and interview, *see* Interview; and intuition, 28-30; law enforcement officers, 48-49; off-beat sources for, 45-46; origins of ideas for, 21-40; and other reporters, 46-48; and patterns, articles inspired by, 30; people as sources for, 42-50; peripheral sources for, 49; principal figure in, 44-45; and records, value of, 50-54; and salvage operations, avoidance of, 93-94; and self-control of reporter, *see* Self-control of reporter; and social functions, 48; sources of information for, 41-58; and stories leading to stories, 31-40; tipsters for, *see* Tipsters; *see also* Case histories; Invasion of privacy; Lawbreaking by reporter; News manipulation; Stories

Jefferson, Thomas, 8
Jones, George, 8

Kennedy, Edward, 88
Kennedy, Joan, 90
Kennedy, John F., 85, 119, 121
Khrushchev, Nikita, 45

Kickback, difficulty of pinning down, 94-95, 96
Ku Klux Klan, 6, 27, 54-58, 116, 123

Ladies' Home Journal, 9
Law enforcement officers, as sources for investigative reporting, 48-49
Lawbreaking by reporter, 133, 138, 139; case history of, 140-42
Lawson, Thomas, 9
Libel, 132
Liberal bias, charge of, 47
Library sources, 52-53
Little, Joan, 49
Louisville Courier-Journal, 135, 136
Louisville Times, 135, 136, 137

McClure's magazine, 8
Manipulation, news, *see* News manipulation
Martindale-Hubbell, 53
Mercer, Lucy, 85
Merrill Lynch, Pierce, Fenner & Smith, Inc., 52
Microphone, and interview control, 73-74
Mills, Wilbur, 85
Mintz, Morton, 9
Moonlighting by reporter, 130-31
More, 3, 139
Muckraking, 8, 9
Mudslinging, 85
My Lai, and Hersh, 9

Nader, Ralph, 9
Nast, Thomas, 8

National Association for the Advancement of Colored People, 50

New York magazine, 1

New York Times, The, 2, 8, 11, 20, 23, 33, 49, 119

News conference, 105-6

News manipulation, 102-26 *passim;* and executive sessions, 113-16; and FBI, 117-19; and national security, involvement of, 119; organized, 105-10; political, case history of, 121-26; reporter included in, 110-11; and setting up reporter, 112-13; and threats by manipulators, 116-17, 120; and trial balloons, 111

News releases, 106-07

News secretaries, 107-10

Nixon, Richard M., 23, 90, 109

Off-the-record material, 74-76

Omaha Sun Newspapers, 33, 34

"Outs" vs. "ins," 24, 26

Pack journalism, pitfalls of, 47

Parole Board files, 133

Patent medicine business, 9

Patterns, articles inspired by, 30

Pearson, Drew, 6, 118

Pentagon Papers, 119, 139

Phillips, David Graham, 9

"Prayer for judgment continued" (PJC), verdict of, 30

Preconceptions, avoidance of, 59-61

Press secretaries, 107-10

Privacy, invasion of, *see* Invasion of privacy

Public records, 51-52

Pulitzer Prize, 1, 19, 21, 34, 41

Quill, The, 118

Quotation: not for attribution, 74; not for direct but for attribution, 74

Ray, Elizabeth, 24, 85

Records, public, 51-52

Redford, Robert, 27

Register of Deeds, 51

Releases, news, 106-07

Reporters Committee for Freedom of the Press, 54

Riegle, Donald W., Jr., 85

Rivers, William, 52

Roalfe, William R., 53

Rockefeller, David, 3

Rockefeller, Nelson, 3

Roosevelt, Franklin D., 85

Roosevelt, Theodore, 8, 9; quoted, 9

Russell, Charles Edward, 9

Sacramento Union, 8

Salisbury, Harrison, 20, 130

Scandalmongering, 83

Secretaries, news, 107-10

Securities and Exchange Commission, 7

Self-control of reporter, 59-63; and demeanor, 61-63; and fairness, 59-61

Sensationalism, 84

Shakespeare, William, 46

Sinclair, Upton, 8

Smith, Doug, 38

Smith, H. Allen, quoted, 135-37
Southern Regional Council, 50
Steffens, Lincoln, 8, 59
Stone, I. F., 9
Stories: evaluation of, 91-92; interview for, *see* Interview; justification for, on basis of evidence, 90-96; leading to stories, 31-40; proof of obtaining, 94-96; reportable, 83-101 *passim;* and salvage operations, avoidance of, 93-94; sources of information for developing, 41-58; *see also* Case histories; Invasion of privacy; Investigative reporting; Lawbreaking by reporter; News manipulation
Sullivan, Mark, 9

Tarbell, Ida, 8
Tax Reform Act, 39
Teapot Dome story, 9
TerHorst, Gerald, 108
Thalidomide, 9
Threats by news manipulators, 116-17, 120
Tipsters: anonymous, 27-28; known, 24-27
To Hell in a Handbasket (Smith), 135
Treason of the Senate, The (Phillips), 9

Trial balloons, 111
Trinity Church (New York), as slumlord, 9
Tweed, Boss, 8
"Two-minute Mile Rule," 71

Unsafe at Any Speed (Nader), 9

Wall Street, and Lawson, 9
Wallace, George, 123, 125
Warren, Robert Penn, 90
"Washington Merry-Go-Round," 118
Washington Post, 1, 3, 24, 47, 51, 85, 137
Watergate, 1, 23, 26, 33, 41, 88, 93, 137, 139
Wegner, Nicholas, 38, 40
White Citizens' Council, 50
Williams, Paul, 33, 39
Woodward, Bob, 1, 7, 23, 45, 52, 63, 139

Xerox Corporation, 130

Ziegler, Ron, 109